The Desert
Gardener's
Calendar

The Desert Gardener's Calendar

Your Month-by-Month Guide

George Brookbank

The University of Arizona Press / Tucson

The University of Arizona Press
Copyright © 1999 The Arizona Board of Regents
First printing
All rights reserved

(∞) This book is printed on acid-free, archival-quality paper.
Manufactured in the United States of America.
04 03 02 01 00 99   6 5 4 3 2 1
Library of Congress Cataloging-in-Publication Data
Brookbank, George, 1925–
The desert gardener's calendar: your month-by-month guide / George
Brookbank.
p. cm.
ISBN 0-8165-1894-7 (pbk.)
1. Gardening—Southwest, New. 2. Desert gardening—Southwest, New.
I. Title
SB453.2.S67B66   1999
635′.0979′09154—dc21
99-26175
CIP

British Library Cataloguing-in-Publication Data
A catalogue record for this book is available from the British Library.

This book is based on month-by-month gardening and landscaping
information from two books by George Brookbank: *Desert Gardening,
Fruits and Vegetables: The Complete Guide* (Fisher Books, 1991) and *Desert
Landscaping: How to Start and Maintain a Healthy Landscape in the
Southwest* (University of Arizona Press, 1992). Used by permission of the
publishers.

Photography by George Brookbank
Edited and designed by Scott Millard
Cover and back cover photos by Scott Millard

Contents

Preface

Each region in the low and middle elevation deserts is different. Get to know the climate of your area, including the particular microclimates—the small climates— that surround your own home landscape.

This book was written with the lower and intermediate deserts in mind, so it should be considered a regional guide. With it comes a warning about connecting horticultural operations to a particular date. It's worth telling you about those warnings.

People coming to live in the desert tend to bring their gardening calendars with them and keep them in their heads. If you've grown up in the Midwest, "spring" is around Memorial Day, but here in the desert it takes place around March 15. Spring in the desert tends to be a sudden, short event and you need to be ready for it. Should you wait for it before beginning your gardening activities, it's possible you won't complete a task before summer arrives.

Newcomers from the colder parts of the country think there is no winter in the desert, but in fact we have enough cold weather, in spite of plenty of sunshine and no snow, to slow down the growth of plants. On winter nights there is even a danger of killing frosts. "Winter" doesn't last long either; in fact, it's not long enough or cold enough to give our deciduous fruit trees and nut trees the chilling they need for productivity.

"Summer" in the desert gives a dormancy to most plants (even desert landscape plants) and there's a need to protect imported, non-native plants from sunburn.

"Fall" is a short period too, and it's the best season for gardeners and landscapers. Unfortunately our mind-set has been conditioned by experience in other places where fall finishes the horticultural year. In the lower deserts it's best to think of fall as a beginning.

Having said all that, there's another awful truth to consider: Any of our seasons can be late or early, mild or severe, longer or shorter than usual. There's no reliability to them, even if you recognize them. And, of course, they don't dramatically start or come to a sudden end on certain dates.

At lower elevations (Yuma at 140 feet above sea level is one example), winter is milder, spring starts earlier, summer lasts longer and is more severe and fall is barely distinct from winter.

As you go "up the hill," planting times are a little later in the year and the seasons seem to separate out a bit more. Summers remain sunny and hot but not as much. Winters last longer and can be more severe.

This altitude effect can be quite localized—a few city blocks, into the next county, or a ways up the road. For example, there are cool places in Tucson down near the rivers because of air drainage. A mile away it's too warm in winter for deciduous fruit trees, yet 20 miles away (and 800 feet higher) in Green Valley the winter is decidedly cooler and spring starts later. In higher elevation regions such as Nogales and Sierra Vista, summers are even cooler, calling for a completely different scheduling.

All this is leading up to us telling you that the information in this book, based on experience in Tucson, should be used as a guide, especially for people living in other parts of the lower desert. Don't take it literally, but make adjustments for your locality, then add in another factor for your elevation. And also remember that Mother Nature will probably fool you anyway.

But you have to start somewhere and we believe that if you use this calendar and let your judgment become more accurate with experience you'll soon be doing everything right. If you start with common sense generalities (less irrigation during the cooler winter months, planting trees and shrubs during the milder fall months, pruning before spring growth starts, mulching the soil surface during the hottest months, as examples) and work toward the more specific and particular tasks according to the seasons, you'll minimize frustrations and maximize your satisfaction. Good luck!

The timing of gardening practices is critical to your success. For example, most wildflowers must be planted in the fall in order to bloom in spring. Seed for these California poppies was sown in early October to produce this March display of flowers.

The Desert Gardener's Calendar

January

January is a quiet time, but you should watch out for frosts and snow. Pay attention to radio and television forecasts. If a warning is issued, cover your plants while they are still warm from the day's sun. In the morning, remove coverings to let the sun warm the plants again.

The bare-root planting season is one of January's traditional events. But it's not the best time to plant—the weather becomes hot and dry in a few months—before plants have enough time to become established. It's usually better to plant from containers in September and October. If you do want to plant bare root, it's not a long season so be prepared for it by having your planting holes dug and ready to receive the trees you buy.

January is a good month for pruning. The leaves have fallen from deciduous trees and you can see the framework of branches. Prune shade trees lightly and try to keep a natural shape. The work done on this tree was minimal. Removing lower branches so the occupants could get in and out of the house was the main goal.

❧ Featured Plants for January

Asparagus

At the end of the month this dormant plant will spring to life. For the next few weeks you can harvest the young spears as they emerge. Prepare to get the most of these harvests by encouraging growth. Cover the bed with a couple inches of steer manure and ammonium phosphate at a rate of 1 pound for every 100 square feet. Apply evenly and water well. Warming temperatures will do the rest, but continue to water regularly for maximum yields.

⚘ Planting

Preparing the Planting Hole

The worse the condition of your soil, the greater the need to dig a large planting hole. There's false economy in skimping at this stage. It's helpful to remove the rocks as you dig, although you'll find tree roots grow around them just as water drains around them. You must dig through any caliche that you find. It may be discouraging, but soften it up by letting a foot of water stand on it overnight. You'll be able to chisel away a few inches thickness the next morning. Keep going in this manner until you have worked your way through it. If you don't, you must expect poor drainage and waterlogged roots in the future. This will cause a decline in tree vigor, and sooner or later, the tree's death.

Enriching the Soil

After you've got all the dirt out of the hole, you put it back. Here's your opportunity to improve the soil by adding three materials: organic matter, sulphur, and ammonium phosphate. If you dig a full-size hole—5 feet deep and 5 feet square—you will need 15 bags of steer manure, 30 pounds of sulphur and 8 pounds of ammonium phosphate.

This should be your standard treatment when you plant any fruit tree in the desert. It improves the soil from a textural and nutrient

standpoint and helps withstand potential attacks from Texas root-rot fungus.

In case you want to dig smaller holes, say for non-native shrubs, here's the formula for the amounts of materials to mix with the soil as you return it to the hole.

Multiply the dimensions of the hole in feet to get its cubic capacity. Divide this by 5 to get the cubic feet of organic matter. You can use peat moss, compost or animal manures. Divide the cubic capacity by 4 to get the pounds of sulphur to add in. Divide by 16 to get the pounds of ammonium phosphate required.

Mix these materials with the soil you took out of the hole; don't make layers. As you backfill, tamp down the soil and water well to encourage it to settle. Plant the tree only after the soil has settled—it may take a couple of weeks. There's nothing as discouraging as watching the soil sink after planting, taking the tree with it.

As you plant, spread the roots in all directions. Plant a bit on the high side, anticipating a slight settling later. You should make sure the bud union is well above soil level. Work in damp soil.

Which Fruit Trees?

Many of our deciduous fruit trees are self-pollinating so only one tree is needed for a harvest. Concentrate on your favorite fruit and plant an early, a midseason and a late variety. Spread the harvest through the season. Plant only what you like to eat.

It's better not to order plants from faraway mail-order places. You can't see what you are buying and their varieties may not be suitable for the desert. Our winters are unusually mild but deciduous fruit trees need a long period of cold. Our summers are dry, hot and sunny. Varieties with a low winter-chill requirement are a must.

An early ripening variety will avoid the damaging green-fruit beetle (see page 83) as well as the heat. If you habitually go away for the summer, there's little point in choosing a variety that fruits during the months you will be absent.

Although the idea of dwarf fruit trees is attractive—we all seem to be living in smaller spaces—those varieties have not been fully tested for desert conditions. Many that have been tested have proven to be disappointing. You can create a dwarf tree merely by pruning hard. For the time being, that's the way to go if you don't have much room.

Get the most out of your fruit trees—make them a part of your landscape. A tree such as an apricot, which has an attractive flower display, should be planted where you will see it. Don't hide it in a distant corner. If you are planting for shade, use a fruit tree and let it grow tall enough for you to sit under. Because of its height, you will lose most of the fruit to birds and beetles.

Allow your trees plenty of room to grow if you have the space. A tree looks small when you buy it but it often grows faster and larger than you can imagine. Provide at least 10 feet of space from a wall, a pathway or another tree. Up to 20 feet would be better, if you have the room. Don't forget to look up. There may be overhead wires and these will require your tree to be cut back later in an unproductive and unattractive manner.

At the nursery, you may find container-grown trees displayed alongside bare-root trees. Both are fine for planting, but you need to be aware of the good and bad points of each.

Buying Quality Bare-Root Trees

The roots are without soil and are exposed. Good gardeners like to look at the roots to make sure they are not twisted or broken, and don't have cankers. Crown gall is a killer. It shows as a knobby, crusty bump on the side of the trunk just below ground level, or on the main root branches. Don't buy crown gall and infect your soil—and lose the tree. Don't buy an old tree that has had its roots cut back to short stubs so it can be planted in a 5-gallon container.

Bare-root trees should be less expensive than those in containers. They were shipped without soil and are sitting in the nursery waiting for a buyer. Overhead is low, but spoilage can be high.

Bare-root trees require good care while waiting for you. The warmth of the desert air, the sunshine and low humidity dry them out. Their roots should be covered in a bin of damp sawdust and they should be sprayed with water frequently. Trees should be stored in the shade to prevent the sunshine from stimulating bud break. Never buy a bare-root fruit tree in bloom or new leaf. It looks great, but it has no reserves to fall back on after it has expended its stored energy on this display.

If you buy a bare-root tree, get it home and plant it as quickly as you can. A good nurseryman will wrap the roots in damp sawdust or sacking and tie a plastic bag around them. Don't go shopping, or visit friends on the way home. The roots must not dry out!

When you get home, take the tree out of its bag and set it in a barrel of water to which you added vitamin B. Let it soak overnight. Prepare the planting hole before fetching the tree for planting. This includes adding backfill soil and amendments as described on page 2.

Buying Quality Container-Grown Trees

Be careful when buying trees in containers. If they have just been put into the container, there's little advantage. Many good roots had to be cut off to get the tree into its 5-gallon home. Ask the nurseryman to split the sides of the container. Someone is going to have to do this anyway, and most nurserymen automatically do it. If the tree has grown in the container for some time, you should see fibrous roots inside of the container and now hold the soil together. Check these small roots. If the container has been sitting out in the hot sun, the roots may be scalded and look brown and soft. The roots should be fresh looking, pale brown or whitish. Dark-brown, soft roots mean something bad happened—perhaps overheating, overwatering, or fertilizer burn. Some trees may be in a container too long and become root-bound. In severe cases roots have been known to grow out of a container's drainage holes and penetrate the soil below. When these are broken by pulling up the container, there's a great loss of roots. Those remaining in the container may not be enough to sustain a large tree. Don't buy these trees.

If you decide to buy a container-grown tree, think roots. Don't buy a tree that has been in the container so long the roots have begun to circle. They can be unraveled at planting, but the tree will never be thrifty. Don't buy a tree with an abnormally thick trunk. It's a sign of old age and old age in a small can isn't worth it.

Don't delay planting. It can become too hot for planting trees, especially bare-root trees, in March. Be an early bird and get it finished during January. The soil will be warm enough to stimulate new root growth, but not hot enough to kill roots. Irrigating will not be so critical. The tree's new shoots will not be so vulnerable to hot drying winds. Plant now, not later!

Although it's too early to plant citrus trees, it's not too early to start digging holes for them. The weather is cool and you can work with enthusiasm. Backfill and let the soil settle until the end of February or the beginning of March.

Trimming the Tree (But Not Citrus)

The bud union is where the tree's top growth was grafted to its roots at the grower. The rootstock is chosen for its vigor and disease resistance, not for its fruit quality. Suckers growing below the bud union should be removed because they are often of poor quality and sap the strength from the upper part of the tree. You can see the bud union quite easily. There's a bend in the trunk and the two parts are often different in color and bark texture.

The top of the tree should be pruned to leave three or four main branches. At the moment, these look like little straws but they will fatten up to produce the main framework limbs. Cut them to leave 10 or 12 inches and try to space them evenly up and around the tree—not all on one side. Remove all the remaining wispy little twigs. For the moment, forget all about fruit production. It will come in three or four years.

Avoid digging a well, which may end up burying the tree. You don't want the bud union to be covered with dirt and weeds as you cultivate in the weeks to come.

⬤ Watering

A couple of days with strong winds quickly dry out a garden and its plants, especially those recently set out. Try to anticipate winds by listening to weather reports. Then give plants an extra watering so they don't suffer. Pay close attention to plants in containers—they dry out a little quicker.

A good late-winter to early spring routine for trees and shrubs is to prepare them for spring growth by giving a liberal irrigation coupled with fertilizer. (See following.) Water out to the ends of the branches and halfway through the irrigation scatter one pound of ammonium sulphate for every 100 square feet. Water until your soil probe reaches to three feet deep. (See photo, page 69.)

Lawns

Cold, wet soil is hard on plants. Don't leave your automatic lawn irrigation system operating on a summer schedule during cold weather. If the soil stays too wet, your plants will be stressed by rhizoctonia organisms, a type of fungus. You'll also discover that a wet lawn can't be mowed easily. Check ryegrass lawns (as well as flowerbeds) with a soil probe to determine if the soil is moist at root level.

Wildflowers

If you sowed wildflower seed in the fall, make sure the plants are receiving water if winter rains are scarce.

⌐ Fertilizing

Don't be alarmed about the red color appearing in the leaves of many plants, from eucalyptus to cabbages to weeds. Cold temperatures bring the color on and it will disappear when it warms up again. The red color is sort of related to low phosphorus in the soil and the inability of plants to get what little is there.

It could be an indication that you should add ammonium phosphate when you next dig your garden or landscaped area in preparation for planting.

Phosphate fertilizer doesn't move through the soil very well, so it's normally a waste to throw it on top of the ground and water it in. You must dig it in! Remember, also, that it's a waste to throw fertilizer at plants that are dormant because of the cold weather.

On the other hand, actively growing plants—including ryegrass lawns and winter vegetables such as lettuce—will respond to an application of the right fertilizer.

During winter, when the soil is cold, a more effective fertilizer is ammonium nitrate. It is soluble in cold water and is carried down by irrigations to the roots of plants. When it is applied to cool-season growers, they readily absorb it. Leafy vegetables, such as cabbage, lettuce and spinach, ryegrass lawns, strawberries and wildflowers benefit from light applications at this time of year.

In addition, large numbers of yellow leaves on trees and shrubs this month tell the tale that buds will soon break into new growth. This is a prime time to supply plants with nitrogen—just prior to new growth.

Sprinkle one-half pound of ammonium nitrate for every 100 square feet of moist soil and water it in. Wash foliage to remove fertilizer from the leaves; it will corrode them if you leave it on. Plants will quickly respond to this fertilizer, even in cold weather.

❊ Pruning

The important task of winter fruit-tree pruning is upon us and cannot be postponed. If we wait until the first sustained warm spell forces new growth, it will be too late for pruning.

If we prune correctly, we will get better production. We are guiding the tree's future growth and keeping it healthy.

There are two basic kinds of pruning. One is to improve the appearance of ornamental trees and shrubs. This is considered corrective or shaping pruning. The other is production pruning—to increase the quality and quantity of a crop. Too many people prune their mulberry trees as if they were peaches, with disastrous results.

Even with the leaves off the tree, there might still be a little sap flow. Check this before you start any pruning by snipping off a twig or two. See whether any sap flows out. It's easily seen as the milky sap of mulberry trees and the clear copious juice of grape. You need to look closer on the ends of apricot and peach twigs. There will always be a little moisture, but satisfy yourself that there is no great sap flow when you snip the branches.

A small, curved, pruning saw is good to have when you find a thick, undesirable limb. Its teeth are set in reverse so you cut wood on the pull stroke, not the push stroke as with a carpenter's saw.

Below left: This is what happens when you prune a shade tree as if it were a deciduous fruit tree. A pruning out encourages new shoots which, in this case, leads to congested growth.

Below: Don't leave long pieces like this. They may sprout lots of short shoots or they may die back. In either case the tree (in this case a mesquite) becomes ugly instead of beautiful. If you have to cut, make your cuts close to the place where the limbs start in order to preserve the natural flow of growth.

Above: Dwarf peach twig on the left should not be cut back as much as the standard variety on the right, otherwise you remove too many fruit buds. It's the number of buds you cut off that matters. The right hand twig has no fruit buds—so all of it goes.

Above right: Grey aphids are a winter problem on vegetables of the cabbage family. If the plants are ready to harvest you don't want to use chemical sprays, so insecticidal soaps (or even household soaps) are better choices for control.

Go easy when pruning shade trees. Try to thin out rather than cut back. But cut away to your heart's content on fruit trees, roses and especially grapes. You can't do a lot of harm. The worst you can do is reduce the crop by cutting too much fruiting wood. You won't kill the tree. Remember that a cut makes for more growth.

Open up the center. Cut back the long branches. Cut the top back to keep the fruit down low. Spray the cut ends before you go to lunch, otherwise you'll forget. It takes only a day for a thick branch end to crack in the dry desert air. Cut close. A lot of stubs left on a pruned tree will result in a lot of extra and congested growth.

Irrigating and fertilizing complement and support pruning. The three make a team for proper growth. Water out as far as the branch spread before they were pruned. Halfway through the watering spread 1 pound of ammonium sulphate for each 100 square feet and continue watering until you can push your soil probe 3 feet into the soil.

Shade trees should not be cut back drastically. Thinning out congested branches may be in order, but it's better to let most trees grow as naturally as possible. Any ornamental shrub that is getting too tall may be "brought down" by cutting the tallest branch where it originates from the plant—perhaps quite low down. Cut it cleanly and treat the cut with pruning paint.

The shoot that was the next lowest is now the tallest, but it is not such a nuisance. You have maintained the natural shape of the plant.

The person who saws everything off the same height is asking for trouble. The result will be bushy new growth from each saw cut that will only get worse as time goes on.

Protect After Pruning

There's some academic controversy as to whether black paint is good for pruned trees in the sunny desert, but years of practical experience show it is safe to use. If you don't protect the cut ends with a spray of pruning paint, the bark can peel back. Bacteria or fungus spores get under the bark and begin to travel down the conducting vessels that carry the sugary sap. Spores are blowing in the wind and are everywhere around us. An infected branch soon shows more dead bark that easily peels to reveal a black sooty material—more spores for more infections. A tree with sooty canker may die in three or four years. If you have any signs of this disease, cut it out while doing your pruning.

Another tree disease encouraged by careless pruning is slime flux. This time it's a bacteria that travels down the conducting vessels, which eventually become gummed up. Pressure forms inside the branch and brown, infected sap is forced out. As it runs out of this weak spot on the branch, it corrodes and kills the bark. It's simple to avoid these diseases. Spray pruning paint on each cut at the ends of the branches as you prune.

Pruning Grapes

Grape planting, pruning and fertilizing can be done in January or February. Grape pruning is special. For one thing it must be done, otherwise the plant grows rampant, becomes a nuisance and produces low yields. Grapes are vigorous plants and for that reason are particularly useful for summer shade.

Before you start pruning, gather some facts. Read, ask questions, attend demonstrations, watch videotapes. Help a knowledgeable friend with his or her pruning. Ask questions and keep him talking. The first time is confusing—but it makes more sense as you gain practice.

Grapes can be cut back to almost nothing. Six spurs, each with four or five buds, means thirty new shoots on just one side of the vine. A total of sixty buds is more than enough for next year's production.

You need to cut a lot—up to 80 percent of last year's growth, leaving about 40 buds to each plant. You cannot kill a grapevine by even the most rigorous pruning, but you can easily set back its production a whole year.

A properly pruned grapevine looks as if it has been worked over by a wild teenager. There's hardly anything left and it seems to have been ruined. Don't worry. Remember, pruning encourages growth. Your grapevine will come back.

Grapevines are pruned to either a spur system or a cane system. Most grape varieties are pruned to a spur system. Your pruned vine appears to have a row of dog teeth to it—short stubs, each with only two buds. Ten spurs on each of the four arms of the vine give you 40 buds. Try to keep them evenly spaced and on top of the arms. There shouldn't be any spurs starting below and hooking upwards.

If you have a Thompson's Seedless or a Black Monukka variety, prune to a cane system. You want two canes on either side of the plant. Each cane will have about ten buds to give you a total of 40 buds as mentioned earlier. The first five or six buds on each cane of these varieties are mere leaf buds. There are no fruit buds until farther out.

Get on with the job of pruning before winter rains and a warm spell start the sap flowing. This will be shown by swelling buds.

Pick up all the pruning and sweep up last year's leaves and throw them away. You don't want powdery mildew to infect the new growth. This fungus survives winters on the canes and is easily recognized by brown patches on 1-year wood. It also rests among the leaf litter. Be clean and tidy.

The ends of pruned grapevines "bleed" profusely, even in cool winters. Pruning paint washes off and you can count the drips as you can with a leaking faucet. Try not to worry. In a day or two the dripping stops unless it has been raining or you have been irrigating unwisely.

Pests and Problems

Grey Aphids

Inspect your broccoli, cabbage and cauliflower plants carefully. Grey aphids may be lurking in their centers. The first indications of something wrong are pale spots on the leaves. On the undersides of these spots you'll find a little cluster of grey, ash-colored aphids. Look tomorrow and the cluster will be twice as large. In a week, the plants will be severely stunted. Spray them with a 50-50 solution of rubbing alcohol and water. A dishsoap-and-water solution, 2 tablespoons to 1 gallon of water, is also effective.

If you use chemical sprays, you cannot eat your vegetables until a period of time has passed after spraying. Read and follow product label instructions before use to be sure they're what you need.

Winter Weeds

Get rid of winter weeds before they become a nuisance. Every flower produces another seven years' plague of seeds. Black mustard and wild barley are currently growing strongly. The first is beginning to flower;

the second is still a refreshing green, but don't be fooled. When wild barley turns dry and brittle, its seeds get into your socks and into your dog's eyes and ears.

It's easy to pull up the young plants, whose roots are shallow during their youth. This is especially true after winter rains that stimulated their growth in the first place have softened the soil. While you are at it, pull up any other weeds such as mallow, shepherd's purse and sowthistle. If you try to pull out these deep-rooted weeds from dry soil, they often break off, leaving their roots to grow new plants again.

Citrus with Thick Skins

Do your grapefruit have thick skins? If so, overfertilizing last year is the cause. Fruit quality is not affected. The grapefruit are still juicy and tasty, even though January is the beginning of the harvesting period. In April, or even May, you'll be more pleased—and perhaps surprised—at the superior taste.

If your fruit has thick skins, especially near the stem end, you can bring up a little trivia at the dinner table and ask your guests if they have any sheep-nosed fruit this year. This is what the "trade" calls such fruit, which are considered undesirable. Forego fertilizing completely this year. The next harvest will be normal.

✓ Special Considerations

Prevent Cold Damage

If the forecast is for cold weather, or if there are several days when the winter sun doesn't shine long enough to warm up frost-tender plants, help them by placing a heat source under each plant so the warmth will rise up through the branches. Keep extension cords, lights, a light blanket or heavy sheet and cardboard boxes handy to cover plants at night. Protecting frost-tender plants for a few selected evenings during the cold season can save years of growth.

If plants are damaged by frost, don't rush to prune them. Leave them alone until warm weather stimulates new buds to sprout. Only then will you know where to cut to remove dead wood.

Snow Tips

Shake snow from junipers, roses, desert broom or other limber-limbed plants in your landscape. It is the weight of snow that causes damage, not the cold. It can injure stiff-branched, young trees, especially if they have poor branch structure.

Allow snow that falls on bedding plants and lawn to melt. It won't harm plants and it usually doesn't last long. But don't walk across a frozen lawn; you'll leave lasting footprints in your wake.

February

*E*very gardening season is different from the last. This is one of the things that makes gardening interesting to experienced gardeners. Just as you are getting used to weather conditions, Mother Nature pulls a fast one and changes things.

Fruit-tree growers don't want a mild winter because they want their trees to get as much chilling as possible. If temperatures remain mild, deciduous fruit trees don't go into full dormancy. A February heat wave causes such trees to flower and sprout leaves before they have had their proper rest. Once this happens there's nothing you can do—you have to go along with it and support that premature growth with a deep irrigation and an application of fertilizer.

A week of warm sunshine in February doesn't mean that spring has arrived. Be prepared for more freezes before your plants can be considered safe. Fruit-tree flowers are delicate and can be killed by a light freeze. If one is forecast, cover your tree at night with a light blanket or a heavy sheet.

Be prepared for a day or two of gusty winds this month. They arrive suddenly, too, and quickly dry out the soil and plants—especially those recently planted. February's weather is undependable. Be on guard!

Bunching onions (multiplying onions is a better name) can be dug and divided this month. As the bunch thickens with new growth, take one or two onions as you need them and leave the bunch in the garden to multiply. A year ago this bunch was a single onion.

❦ Featured Plants for February

Citrus

Although citrus trees are evergreen, leaves do not remain on the tree forever. Evergreen trees are always dropping their leaves—look under pine trees for such evidence.

When a leaf gets old, it gives up its nitrogen, which makes it turn yellow. The nitrogen is taken back into the tree and redistributed to the growing parts—the new shoots at the ends of the branches—that are, at this time of year, beginning to break out. If a lot of new growth breaks out, a large amount of nitrogen is drawn from the older leaves, causing many to turn yellow.

You can gauge the nutrient status of your tree by measuring the number of yellow leaves against the amount of new shoots breaking out. If things are too yellow, it helps to apply a nitrogenous fertilizer. Use ammonium nitrate at this time of year because you want a quick nitrate uptake of nutrients. You should prevent the rapidly growing new shoots from being starved.

Apply a small amount—say, one-half pound of ammonium nitrate to each 100 square feet—under the spread of the branches. Be sure there is plenty of moisture in the soil before you scatter fertilizer under the tree.

Citrus trees are supposed to sweep to the ground when mature. This bothers a lot of new gardeners. It's really better to let them sweep to the ground because that's where most of the fruit is produced in the early years. Avoid imitating people who trim their trees to make them look like lollipops on a white stick. If you allow a tree to grow naturally, the sun can't reach the trunk, so there's no need to paint it white.

Don't worry about those brown leafless branches on the insides of a citrus. They are not dead. Don't prune them—they have leaves, and fruit, on their outer ends.

Onions

The best way to grow onions—after you've selected a suitable variety— is to sow seeds in boxes in September, transplant seedlings into the garden during January or February and harvest in May. Two good onion varieties are Texas Grano and California Red. Both are *short-day* types. This means they are suited to regions closer to the tropics where days are short—rather than northern states where summer days are long. They are also quick to mature. Be forewarned that varieties that grow well in the desert don't usually keep well.

Don't plant a large number of bulbing onions. They need a lot of time to reach harvest stage and take up a lot of garden space. Plus the one-time harvest must be eaten in a short amount of time. By contrast, the many kinds of bunching onions, also called *everlasting, multiplying* or *dividing onions,* provide tasty harvests throughout most of the year. One little bulb quickly grows into a clump and you can eat the green leaves, young tender bulbs and ripe, firm bulbs as you need them. (See photo at left.) Harvest a few, replant a bulb or two and the onion garden seems to go on forever.

After a rake is used for initial leveling, a trickle of water shows the gardener where the low spots are. These can then be filled in with soil from the high parts.

Woody crop residues, in this case corn stalks, should not be dug into the soil but taken to the compost pile where they will decompose. The big clumps of freshly dug soil in the background are ready for a heavy sprinkling of steer manure or decayed compost, blended with ammonium phosphate and soil sulphur.

Soil Preparation

It's important to prepare the soil before planting a vegetable garden. Follow these steps:

Dig deeply as you prepare the soil. Remove any overwintering chrysalids of cabbage-white butterflies, grape-leaf skeletonizers or squash-vine borers. Take out the white grubs, too. Here is your chance to get rid of nutgrass that lies deep in the soil as hard round nuts held to one another by slender threads. It's dormant now, but it's a bear in the summer garden. It's worse than Bermudagrass because it is more resistant to chemical weedkillers. Pull out both of these summer nuisances as you dig. A fork does a more thorough job than a spade because it combs out long runners, whereas a spade cuts them into smaller pieces, each capable of growing again.

Thoroughly dig in organic matter using 2 or 3 inches of compost or steer manure with 3 pounds of ammonium phosphate and 5 pounds of soil sulphur for each 100 square feet of garden.

Each time you work the soil, dig down to that undisturbed layer of a redder color and mix in an inch of it. This is a good way to deepen your garden soil gradually. Don't bring up too much poor subsoil at once. You'll reduce the soil's fertility if you do.

Shaping the Planting Bed

Rake the soil over to level it and shape a bed as long as you like, but no wider than 4 feet with a pathway of 2 feet between beds. You want to reach the middle of the bed to weed and to harvest without treading on the soil. You should be able to push a wheelbarrow along the pathway without brushing against plants. When laying out a first-time garden, give yourself and your plants plenty of elbow room.

Shape the bed with a rim around it about 3 inches high so water will not run off when you flood the bed. Don't build ridges because they dry out too quickly and draw salts to the plants. Ridges dry out nicely in places where the rainfall is heavy. In a dry desert, they dry out too quickly.

The bed with its new organic matter and fertilizer should be allowed to mellow for a week or so before you set out plants or sow seeds. If you are early with this task, so much the better. You could even cover the bed with a sheet of clear plastic to germinate any weed seeds present in the soil.

Scuffle any germinating weed seedlings, but make sure you leave the soil surface absolutely level. Then you will be able to flood the bed evenly to get vegetable seeds to germinate or plants to take hold. High spots in a bed mean dry spots; low places mean too much moisture. An uneven bed means uneven growth in your plants and a waste of water.

Compost

All this soil preparation will have used up your old compost, but the new pile calls for your attention. Turn the pile of decaying leaves and refuse accumulated from last fall. If a lot of steam comes off the compost, you'll know bacterial activity is taking place and all is well. On the other hand, no heat means no activity—no activity means no decomposition. Winter rains are usually sufficient to encourage bacteria to go to work. If the pile is dry, sprinkle the leaves with water as you turn and aerate them.

At this time of year kitchen scraps include citrus rinds. They make excellent compost.

Planting

Arbor Day Tree Planting

Arbor Day is a reminder to plant a tree and enjoy nature—a sort of Rite of Spring that relieves the monotony of grade-school life. There are two Arbor Days in Arizona. For the warm, lower-elevation desert areas it's the first Friday in February. For the higher elevations where they have a simple, summer-and-winter gardening system, it's the first Friday in April. It's a sensible adjustment from the conventional dates used in the East, which would not be appropriate for the desert. The two-day approach also tells us that the desert is not a vast, uniform region. Although it is uniformly dry, elevation greatly affects the timing of gardening operations. Don't plant the traditional fir or elm but, instead, consider a native tree, or pecan, citrus or even a deciduous fruit tree— providing it has not leafed out already.

With water becoming more expensive as the years go by, it makes sense to get the most out of any tree you plant. An ideal tree can supply shade in summer, allow sunshine in during the winter months, have a nice appearance, as well as produce colorful flowers and something to eat.

Vegetable Seeds: Speeding Germination

If you want to intrude on Mother Nature and get things going a little earlier than she allows, try covering the ground with clear plastic. Sunlight passing through the plastic will warm up the soil to your advantage.

Make shallow trenches in your garden, running north and south, about 2 inches deep and 6 inches wide. Sow seeds in the bottom of the trenches. Lettuce, radish, turnip, beet or any of the quicker-growing winter vegetables work well. Lay the plastic sheet on the ground over the trenches and hold it down with bricks in case the wind wants to blow it away.

Moisture evaporating from the soil condenses on the underside of the plastic and drips back. Germination is rapid and the seedlings stay moist.

If you expect summer weeds to be a nuisance, use clear plastic to pregerminate their seeds and get them out of the way before you plant tomatoes, bell peppers, corn, squash and melons. Wet the ground, dig it and cover your garden area with a sheet of clear plastic. Anchor it at the edges with bricks. The sun will do the rest. In about three weeks there will be a mass of tender green weeds that can be dug into the soil as green manure together with compost, ammonium phosphate and soil sulphur in the usual manner. If you have Bermudagrass, nutgrass, then you should not dig it in again because it will merely multiply. Dig the ground with a fork and pick out the young plants. (See page 66.)

Planting Winter Vegetables

A February planting of winter vegetables, which will grow until April or May, competes for garden space with a March planting of summer tomatoes, squash, corn and peppers. To overcome the dilemma, an energetic gardener really needs two gardens—one for a February planting of root and leaf crops that will take up space until they are harvested in May—the other for a mid-March planting of summer vegetables that will occupy the ground until fall.

If you are short on garden space, you can set out plants or sow seeds of winter vegetables in black-colored containers.

Put the containers in a sunny place where their black sides gather heat from the sun, which warms the soil inside and stimulates the roots to grow vigorously. You'll get a rapid return this way and you can measure the difference by comparing lettuce plants in the containers with a half dozen set out in the soil at the same time. In a recent cool spring, lettuce plants in containers were three weeks earlier—a worthwhile difference. Containers smaller than 5-gallon buckets require more frequent watering. Plants become rootbound rather quickly, too.

You can also speed up your harvest of leafy vegetables by giving frequent applications of nitrate fertilizers. Ammonium nitrate and calcium nitrate are freely soluble in water, so they reach down to the plants' roots easily. Plants absorb nitrogen in the nitrate form, so these fertilizers are ready to use—they are the fast foods of the plant world.

A hose proportioner can be used to apply nitrate fertilizers at the rate of 1 tablespoon to 1 gallon of water. Do it once a week or so, until the leaves become dark green. Afterwards, fertilize about every two weeks.

Planting Vegetables in Bags of Soil Amendment

Another way to get a quick harvest of winter vegetables during a spring that isn't warming up fast enough is to grow the vegetables in plastic bags of soil amendment. Go to a nursery and buy large bags of forest mulch, grow mix or whatever it is called locally. Don't buy steer manure because you are going to plant young plants directly in the mixture. Steer manure will burn the roots.

Lay the bags in a sunny place, preferably on a board because you may want to move them later. Make sure there are drainage holes at the bottom of the bag—which was its side when you read the label in the nursery. Then wrap a sheet of black plastic round the bag, tucking it underneath without blocking the drainage holes.

Press and shape the top of the bag so it is flat. Use a cookie cutter to make eight holes through both pieces of plastic on the top of the bag. Slowly pour water through these holes until the bag is well soaked and water is coming out the drainage holes. Now you are ready to plant through the plastic into the soil mix.

There will be a minimum of evaporation from the bag. The only moisture loss will be through drainage and plant use. However, keep an eye on the plants and prevent them wilting by timely waterings. In a

During the winter months shadows are longer, which means the soil stays colder. Try to avoid planting in such spots in your yard. Winter vegetables need sunshine.

couple of weeks time, after they have become established, you may include a tablespoon of houseplant food in the water to nourish the plants and get them growing quickly. But it will be the warmth of the sun—captured by the black plastic—that speeds up their growth.

After you harvest the vegetables, don't throw away the bag of material. Dig it into your next garden. What a saving!

Vertical Gardens: Space-Saving Planting

Another way to get a lot from a little is to make your garden grow as vertical as possible. After all, air space is free and it goes on for a long way. Make plans now to use it in your gardening program. Prepare the soil along your chainlink fence.

Garden peas and snow peas lend themselves to vertical gardening. And cucumbers can be grown on strings up to 6 feet high. In the summer, many kinds of melons, winter squash and tomatoes can be grown upward instead of outward.

Watering

If it doesn't rain this month, you must irrigate. This becomes more important as the weather warms and plants start to grow again. Use your soil probe to tell you when to water. Don't forget to water the wildflowers. Annual wildflower plants will die if the weather turns warm and the soil is allowed to dry. Irrigate them so moisture reaches 6 inches deep into the soil. This encourages deep roots, helping produce a long display of color in March or April.

Give dormant plants a good watering in early February. This is a critical month for all dormant plants, especially trees and shrubs—the warming weather stimulates buds to swell and break into leaves and flowers. Now is the time to fertilize, too. (See following.) Keep in mind that ammonium nitrate is more concentrated and works faster in cold soil than does ammonium sulphate.

Fertilizing

Citrus Trees

Everything has to be done at the right time, but the right time often sneaks up on you—especially in the spring. The secret to success lies in being ready for what may come next.

The February application is best given before new shoots break out. Ammonium sulphate, spread over the surface of the soil and watered in with a deep irrigation, takes time to be changed into a nitrate form. This is absorbed by the tree's roots, carried up the trunk, moved through the branches and out to the ends of the twigs where the new growth is starting.

If growth started while you weren't looking, the big question is whether to fertilize later or skip it. The answer depends on the tree's appearance. If the leaves are dark green, don't fertilize this time. If the leaves are generally pale, give a fertilizer application, even if you are late. Don't take any notice of a few bright-yellow leaves—these are old ones dying and ready to drop off. Don't fertilize flowering trees but you must irrigate them because they need water to fill the new growth.

Here are some tips on how to fertilize a tree:

Flood the soil underneath the spread of the branches, keeping the water confined by a little bank or berm scraped up from outside the tree's dripline. When you can push your soil probe 18 inches into the water-softened soil, turn off the faucet. Now scatter ammonium sulphate evenly, at the rate of 1 pound to every 100 square feet, onto the moist soil. Open up the faucet again and continue watering until your soil probe easily goes down 3 feet.

The latter half of the irrigation carries the fertilizer down to the root zone that was premoistened by the first half. It's always a mistake to apply dry fertilizer to dry soil and then water it in. The surface roots may be burned with too strong a solution of fertilizer.

Pruning

Frost-Damaged Plants

Don't be in a hurry to prune any plants that were damaged by an earlier frost—even if they look terrible. We may get another frost! Wait until spring has really arrived and the tree has put out new shoots, telling you which branches were killed. Then make cuts just behind the dead parts to encourage side shoots where you want them to fill in an empty space in the plant's framework.

A normal, healthy citrus tree is seldom pruned. Even a light trimming of the outer foliage takes away next year's crop because flowers are developed at the ends of branches. For this reason, most gardeners let their citrus trees grow to a natural shape—even if the lower branches sweep the ground.

There is an exception to this practice. Lemon trees grow vigorously this time of year. You can prevent their shoots from getting too long if you give each one a "soft pinch." All you need for a soft pinch is to squeeze the branches between your finger and thumbnail. (Some gardeners keep their nails long and sharp for this springtime operation.) Pinch an inch of soft growth off the ends of strong shoots before they get 5 or 6 inches long. This makes the tree more compact because side shoots develop behind the pinch. New side shoots eventually produce fruit.

Pests and Problems

A warm February will bring out insects—good and bad—and you will see both of them on your plants. The good ones are, of course, bees that are busy working the flowers. The bad ones are tiny and barely noticeable. They are called thrips, and they rasp on the surface of fresh new leaves for the juices. One or two thrips have no effect, but they seldom come in ones and twos.

You don't see thrips damage until two or three months later. The new leaves—much larger now—are twisted and misshapen. Such leaves function well, they only look horrible.

Bolting to Seed

When vegetable plants run amok, they're useless. Spurts of warm

A pruning cut is an open wound. If sticky sap is flowing, it provides an entry point for bacteria and fungi. If infected, the inside wood, as well as the bark on the outside, can become corroded and die. Use a spray can of pruning paint immediately after making cuts to prevent such losses.

This is a good method to tie any green landscape tree or fruit tree to a stake during its early years. Several turns of soft cotton rope hold the tree away from the stake in a loose but protective cradle.

weather cause the staid cabbage, lettuce and even carrots and beets, to flower instead of continuing to develop leaves or roots. This is called *bolting to seed*. It's a natural reaction to the end of winter at a time of their development when they are halfway through their life.

When there are sudden warm spells in February—a gradual increase in temperature doesn't affect matters—you had better be ready for a disastrous turn of events in the winter garden.

Cabbage plants that are coming along nicely develop a crack in the topmost part of the head, revealing the pale, tightly packed leaves inside. At this point you can and should harvest the crop before things get worse. Salvage the crop before the flower stalk pokes out.

Lettuce does it a little differently and it's not as easy to detect. The leaves look good and they stay fairly tight, but when you get them in the salad bowl they have a bitter taste and are inedible.

Root crops—beet, carrot and turnip—also surprise you. Only rarely can you salvage their harvest because the roots become woody and inedible as soon as the flower stalks begin to show.

Special Considerations

Newly Planted Trees

New trees will need staking to save them from being blown over by spring winds that are soon to arrive. Don't tie a tree's trunk tightly to the stake. Use a soft cotton rope to make a loose figure-of-eight between the stake and the trunk. (see photograph, opposite.) A loose tie allows the tree to flex in a light wind but secures it in a storm. Install two or three of these ties evenly spaced along the length of the trunk for proper support.

Mistletoe

In winter you can see things that were hidden by summer foliage, such as infestations of parasitic mistletoe in desert trees. Mistletoe is a green plant, and as such uses the sun's energy for growth, but it also saps the host tree's energy by stealing nutrients from the branches. Mistletoe doesn't steal a lot of nutrients from its host, but a heavy infestation will shade a tree's leaves. It's best to remove it when you see it. A long hooked pole is right for the job; just pull the parasite off. If you cut the branch to which the mistletoe is attached, you run the risk of spoiling the natural beauty of the tree. If mistletoe grows back, pull it off again. Don't use weedkillers on mistletoe. It and its host are closely connected and share a common source of moisture and nutrients. You'll poison the tree, as well.

For chronic infestations that have been going on for a few years, the roots of the mistletoe may cause the host branch to thicken, making removal difficult. Pull off the mistletoe then wrap black plastic around the swollen area on the branch. Tie the ends loosely, but the plastic should block the covered area from all exposure to light. The new mistletoe shoots will perish in the darkness. (See photo, page 148.)

Newly Planted Annuals

Spring winds are common this month. They can quickly dry out the

shallow roots of recently planted annuals. In addition, wind-blown sand can damage plants. Pay close attention to water needs, and supply shelter to such plants during windy periods.

New Plants from Cuttings

When people trim their roses, grapes, figs, pyracantha and oleanders, they are often interested in starting new plants from the trimmings. It seems a shame to throw away all that good stuff. Cuttings can be made from these trimmings and no special equipment is necessary, but it calls for close attention for a year or more if you are to finish with sturdy plants. If you have a greenhouse or a cold frame where you can keep the temperature at 75F and maintain high humidity, it will be a lot easier.

Should you admire a particular plant belonging to your neighbor and want one just like it, try your hand at making cuttings. Or there may be a time when you need many plants. Perhaps you want to start a long hedge and think you can save money by creating your own plants. Or the nurseries cannot find a particular plant for you. With these situations you could well be ahead by making your own plants and you may enjoy the exercise, too. However, under normal circumstances it's more expedient and less expensive to purchase plants from a nursery, where there is a wide selection. You'll also be getting plants ready to put in the ground immediately.

Plants developed from cuttings have a fibrous root system as opposed to a tap root from a seedling and are therefore suitable for growing in half barrels and other large containers where root room is restricted. Move the cuttings from small containers into larger ones as the roots become crowded.

Preparing a Soil Mix

To start cuttings prepare a soil mix by using equal parts of sand, perlite, peat moss and vermiculite. Don't add in any fertilizers or steer

During the winter months when trees have dropped their leaves, mistletoe becomes obvious. It's a parasite that weakens a tree by stealing its nutrients in the spring and by shading its leaves in the summer. Get rid of it by pulling it off. Don't leave the pieces lying around or birds will harvest and spread the berries.

February
In Your Garden

manure because they burn young, delicate tissues.

Don't try to root cuttings in water. Even if you are successful, the roots are weak and usually break when you plant them in soil. It's too much of a shock for the plant when you move it from a water medium into a soil medium.

Use any container larger than a pint size with drainage holes punched in the bottom. Large styrofoam coffee cups are readily available and inexpensive, but they are narrow at the base and tend to tip over when watered.

Tip cuttings grow quickest. You find these at the ends of branches. Their growing point is indicated by lots of small fresh leaves.

From this single growing point, new leaves emerge to make your new plant. You don't want very soft green twigs, but something with a bit of rigidity to it. Pyracantha, for example, doesn't have much tender growth and grape cuttings are usually taken when the plant is leafless.

Where to Cut the Cutting

To obtain a more woody cutting, cut lower down the branch where the bark is a darker color and the stem is thicker. These woody cuttings don't root so readily, or grow as quickly as do tip cuttings. However, they develop into a bushier plant because new growth comes from the side buds instead of a single terminal bud. The terminal bud was removed when you made the first cut to get a tip cutting. The farther down you go on the branch, the more woody the material becomes and the harder it is to grow a new plant successfully.

Planting Cuttings

No matter what the age of the wood you select, make the cutting about 5 or 6 inches long. Remove the lower leaves. Dip the lower end in RooTone® powder before the cut dries out. Tap the cutting on the edge of the table to remove excess powder, then quickly but gently poke the stem into the soil mix.

Use a pencil to make a hole in the mix. This will allow you to plant each cutting at about the same depth without scraping off the RooTone® as the cutting is inserted. Place a cutting in each container with 2 or 3 inches of it buried in the soil mix.

Water and set in a warm, sunny place. Sunshine helps, but it's the warmth of the soil that determines whether you get quick root growth or not.

Provide Warmth and Moisture

If you are planning to buy any equipment, make the first item a soil-heating cable. Spread the cable out and cover it with a sheet of metal. Then place the containers on the warm metal. Warm soil makes roots grow, even if the air temperature is cold.

Keep the soil mix moist. Reduce transpiration by grouping several containers close together. If leaves are large and numerous and during periods of hot, dry weather, cutting off half of each leaf when you make the cutting will reduce moisture lost through transpiration.

A plastic wrap around the cuttings or a plastic bag over the container and its cutting also retains moisture. Be careful that this doesn't develop such a moist and still environment around the cuttings that fungus and bacterial rots begin to thrive.

The best time to make cuttings is when, or just before, the plant comes into a flush of growth. This coincides with the usual pruning times in spring and fall. Cuttings taken at other times grow more slowly and require more care.

Keep your cuttings well watered, especially during dry, windy periods. Although you don't want the soil to remain wet for any period, it is hard to overwater an open, free-draining soil mix.

Inspect the soil from time to time by poking a wooden stick into the bottom of the container to see if it comes out too wet.

Remember that a cutting already has leaves, is active, and is unsupported by a root system for at least ten weeks. Sometimes a cutting will grow new leaves without the benefit of roots. Don't disturb things by picking cuttings out of the soil to see what is happening.

Moving to a Larger Container

After a few weeks, turn the container upside down and give a sharp tap to dislodge the soil. Before the young roots begin to go round and round at the bottom of the container, it's time to transfer the cutting to a larger container. Good-size roots will hold moist soil together during this operation, but work quickly and calmly.

Start adding Miracle-Gro® to the water just before the moving up operation. A teaspoon to 1 gallon of water is all your plants need. A week or two after the moving up, increase the dose to 1 tablespoon to 1 gallon. If the leaf color becomes dark green, water with plain water.

There's little value in misting your cutting unless you use distilled water. A misting with salty water puts salts on the leaves and the tender growing points. This causes growth to stop and sometimes it's the death of the cutting.

Take more cuttings than you think you'll need. Seldom does even a skilled gardener get 100 percent take. Don't take cuttings from a diseased plant—you will be propagating the disease as well.

Some plants that easily root from cuttings with the first being easier than the last are: grape; fig; oleander; tomato; lemon and lime; cottonwood, geranium; desert willow; sweet potato; privet; rose; grapefruit; orange and tangerine; peach and apricot; apple and pear.

March

March is often a confusing month for gardeners. We get promising periods of warm, sunny weather followed by sharp, cold spells, followed by warm weather again. Often there are gentle rains.

The first warm days of March bring ants out from their rest beneath the soil, gophers and squirrels become active again, the birds sing, bees gather nectar, people are at work on their rooftop coolers, and construction workers take off their shirts—but these signs are not reliable. A more trustworthy (but not infallible) sign is the appearance of mesquite flowers, the long, yellow blooms that hang from the twigs like catkins. After mesquite flowers appear, it's usually summer all the way.

Although we may get several false starts before the real summer, every warm spell causes plants to grow. The danger is that there might still be a late frost, so don't be hasty in planting your summer vegetables.

❧ Featured Plants for March

Fruit Trees

Flowers on fruit trees may have already faded and young fruit are apparent. Early varieties are almost sure to have done this and now it is the turn of the later peaches and citrus. Be especially careful at such times. A warm spell should remind us to irrigate fruit trees. If we forget, the tree will be under stress when it is trying to develop fruit. The fruit readily falls off when the tree is under stress.

There's a misunderstanding about the care of fruit trees at blossoming time. No matter what you hear, follow this simple guideline—keep the tree well watered and don't apply fertilizer. It can act as a shock on the tree's system, especially if too much is given at one time. It is often enough of a shock to cause the tree to drop young fruit.

Don't spray your trees for citrus thrips—or nectarine thrips, for that matter—because you will kill good insects that pollinate the flowers of your trees. If the flowers are not pollinated (because you killed the pollinators), you won't get a crop.

A caution worth repeating: Water well to support the growth of flowers and leaves. Once they have started coming out you mustn't stop watering. It's highly likely those recent rains didn't reach very deep into the soil.

Apples, apricots and peaches can be seen behind the faded flowers. If there are a lot of them, you will have to do some thinning. It's not easy to do because you are rubbing out a part of the harvest. If you are a knowledgeable gardener, you know some of the fruit is going to fall off on its own and some might be naturally thinned by dry winds, a late frost, shortage of water or other stressful conditions.

Just do it—or get your neighbor to thin your fruit and you thin his. If juvenile fruit remains on the tree, you'll harvest a heavy crop of little fruit. The tree will exhaust itself to accomplish this and likely will produce a light harvest the next year.

Grapefruit get their name from their grapelike, clustering growth. In March the fruits are getting sweeter and will continue to improve in April and even into May. Eat one every day to get your vitamin C.

Olives and Mulberries: No Flowers, No Fruit

Some people don't like fruit to develop on their olive trees. As the fruits ripens and falls onto sidewalks and concrete patios they can leave stains. If you don't like olive fruit, destroy the flowers and young fruit by spraying them with a solution called Olive-Stop®, available at nurseries. Follow directions on the product label. Spray the tree all over, wetting the flowers. Because olive trees flower over a period of time, it's advisable to make three or four sprayings to catch the first blooming, the middle periods and the final blooming. This spraying will also be helpful to people who suffer from pollen irritation. You can use the same product to destroy the male flowers of mulberry.

To get your olive tree to produce bigger olives, allow the first flowers develop into fruit, then spray the second and third waves of flowers with Olive-Stop®. This eliminates competition and the first fruits grow bigger. Your tree must have the natural potential to produce big fruit. Some kinds are genetically small fruited; they'll never give large fruit no matter what you do.

Most of the mulberry trees used in landscaping are males, which produce pollen but no fruit. In years past, people disliked the pavement stains made by falling fruit, so gardeners often shunned female trees. Now the poor mulberry is blamed for springtime nose sniffles. You can reduce pollen by spraying the flowers (at the stage shown above) with water. This knocks the pollen to the ground.

❧ Planting

Good gardeners have their ground all prepared and are ready for planting. However, they are not seduced by the first warm spell that comes along—even if there are fresh young plants in the nurseries. They know unsettled conditions are a normal start to the summer season and they wait for the soil to warm up sufficiently. They might even use a soil thermometer poked in the ground to register the temperature at root depth. It's best to wait until the soil reaches 50F before planting tomatoes, the first of the summer vegetables to go in the ground.

If you are hasty and plant too early, you will discover that there is often no merit in it. An early planting in cold soil is quickly overtaken by a later planting in warm soil. Don't wait too long, though. There aren't too many days of good growing weather before late June when it gets too hot for pollination of summer vegetables such as corn, peppers and tomatoes.

Selecting Plants for Planting

If you have grown your own plants from seed, choose the healthiest ones and throw the others away. There's little point in starting with poor material. If you buy at the nursery, be picky about your purchases. Some plants may have been on the shelves a long time. Closely examine the roots in their tiny compartments. If they are crowded, soft and black, ask to see the latest shipment. Examine the roots; they should be pale and fuzzy, not crowded. Don't be too shy to ask. A good nurseryman will respect your concern about getting healthy plants.

Look at the leaf color. If the leaves are pale green, the plants are suffering from a shortage of nitrogen. This nutrient was washed out of the soil mix by watering while the plants were waiting to be purchased. Most nurserymen are reliable when it comes to watering their bedding plants, but it's an unwelcome expense to supply plants with fertilizer while at their stores. Their business is to sell plants, not look after them as if they were in gardens. Nor do they want their plants to grow too big.

When you finally get your plants in the ground—and the weather is still cool—cover them with a glass jar. This gives each plant its own greenhouse. Remove the jars if the weather is turning warm at midday. Push the jars into the soil and you'll protect plants from surface-crawling cutworms. (See page 127.)

Hitchhikers on Nursery Tomato Plants

Before you buy tomato plants from a nursery, inspect them closely.

Below: Cold winds can delay plant growth, so fend them off and capture the sun's heat with a temporary plastic shelter.

Below right: Remove the bottom of a glass jar to make an individual greenhouse for each newly planted plant. It will encourage rapid growth during cold spells before warm spring weather arrives.

They may be hiding aphids—little black pests that suck juices from the plant. Get rid of them by spraying with a 50-50 solution of rubbing alcohol and water, or spray with a soap and water solution—2 tablespoons of dishwashing soap mixed with 1 gallon of water. If you like, you can buy insecticidal soap from a nursery. And, if you want to use something a lot stronger, consider applying Malathion 50® or diazinon.

Planting Tomatoes

Summer will be on us soon, and the end of June is going to be unfailingly hot. We want our plants to be well established before this happens so they'll be able to take the heat. The dilemma is that the soil isn't warm enough. Here's the trick to overcome that problem.

Remove the lower, older, yellowing leaves of your newly purchased tomato plant. There may even be some bumps on the stem. These are *adventitious roots*, a fancy name for additional roots that appear where we least expect them—in this case, on the lower stem. We are going to put these bumps to good use.

Dig the planting hole in the normal way to accommodate the roots of the young plant. Make a sloping trench so you can lay the plant on its side so the leaves will rest at soil level. In a day or two the top will have straightened itself up and the plant will look as it if had been buried—which it has. However, the true roots will be in the upper warm soil, along with the bumpy stem. Your plant will soon have additional *adventitious* roots growing from the bumps.

If you had set the plant upright and buried it up to its neck of leaves, its roots would be deep in the soil. This soil is colder compared to the upper layer of soil. This greatly slows root growth until the weather and soil have warmed considerably.

Another way to encourage new plants is to water them in with a starter solution. This is discussed on page 43.

If cold weather follows planting, cover each plant with a 1-gallon glass jar. It will act as an individual greenhouse. When it is pushed into the soil, it also provides a protection from cutworms. These caterpillars spend the day in the soil and at night wander around to look for plant stems to chew.

Be ready to remove the glass jars if the weather warms up, then replace them if it turns cold. Opaque plastic jars are not as effective as clear glass jars.

Encourage Growth

The name of the game this time of the year is "get them growing." Any cold period will check growth. This is even more applicable to bell peppers and eggplant—plants that like a little more heat than tomatoes.

Seeds of corn and squash also need help if the weather turns cold. Spread clear plastic sheeting on the soil between the rows or around the clusters of plants if you sow in groups. This will get the most from the spring sunshine. Your goal at the beginning of the season is to grow roots. This is best achieved in a warm soil, even if air temperatures are cool. After three or four weeks, pull up this plastic and store it to use again in the fall when the weather cools.

Protect newly planted shrubs and new leaf growth from wind with a temporary screen. If you have just moved into a brand new subdivision that has no shelter, it's worth setting up a length of four-foot-high snow fence. If you want greater protection, fasten sheets of plastic on the windward side.

💧 Watering

March is a time of gusty winds, first from one direction bringing humidity from the California coast—then dry, dusty winds from the east. These winds can shock plants and you must be ready to act to prevent plant roots from drying out. When watering trees and shrubs, provide deep irrigations that reach to 3 feet deep. Use the soil probe to be certain how deep moisture is reaching. Dull and bluish leaves indicate that a plant is short of water. Plants that have just been set out are particularly at risk so be ready with the garden hose. March showers are welcome, but don't rely on them to give your plants the water they need to make rapid growth. Pay close attention to plants in containers. Container soil dries out quickly, and plants must have adequate moisture if they are to grow and flower.

Flowering fruit trees need water, not fertilizer. Flowers are delicate and are easily damaged if they become too dry; their stalks break and the wind blows them away. Flower stalks also break if the tree is fertilized during flowering; it's too much of a shock. Fertilizer at this time can cause young fruit to drop, too.

As top growth of fruit trees occurs in the spring so does root growth under the soil. It's important to water that new root growth, so now's the time to widen the irrigation circle by drawing soil from outside. Don't dig a deep well beneath plants or you may chop young roots.

Ryegrass Lawns

Rains in March, coupled with warming temperatures, make ryegrass lawns grow vigorously. You'll have to mow more frequently, perhaps every five days. Don't let ryegrass get away from you; keep it at 2 inches high. If there's a dry, hot spell in March, the ryegrass will suffer from the heat and the underlying Bermudagrass will come out of dormancy. Now, there's great competition between the two grasses and you can work this to your advantage. If you want to encourage the Bermudagrass in anticipation of summer, mow the lawn as close to the ground as you can. This will weaken the struggling ryegrass. The operation also will expose Bermudagrass thatch, a layer of dead leaves and stalks, so you can get rid of it. Removing it by hand is a lot of work. Consider renting a power machine, called a dethatcher or verticutter, to do the job. After dethatching, irrigate well and fertilize.

One advantage of taking out the thatch in March, while it's cool, is that the soil does not burn. Dethatching during summer allows the strong sunshine to kill the exposed Bermudagrass roots, especially on high spots in the lawn.

Fertilizing

Foliar Feeding

New spring growth is tender and absorbent. If a tree is short of fertilizer, it can be fed through the young leaves. You make a mild solution, usually a tablespoon of fertilizer to a gallon of water, and spray the leaves thoroughly. You need to buy a special "foliar feeding" fertilizer. Don't use your ordinary garden fertilizer. Foliar feeding is a common practice with grapes and pecans, both of which frequently suffer from a shortage of zinc.

Grapes will be ready for the treatment now, but pecans leaf out a little later. Apricots, citrus and peaches can be fed in this manner as long as their leaves are fresh.

Zinc Deficiency

If your trees have little leaves or if your pecans have soft, dark meats, zinc is probably the missing element. Spray with zinc sulphate, which is available at nurseries. There are specialized formulations of other chemicals, but you can take care of the common shortages by using a balanced houseplant fertilizer containing a range of nutrients. It's a shotgun approach to any particular shortage but if you are going to spray for zinc, you might just as well spray for copper and manganese and anything else at the same time. This is especially useful if you know some element is missing but are not sure which one. The deficiency symptoms are remarkably confusing, even to experts.

New leaves stay absorbent for about a month, and new leaves continue to appear. Nutrient spraying may be done every week in the spring for three or four sprayings.

It seems contradictory to apply salts deliberately even as plant fertilizers when we always try to avoid letting sprinklers spray plant foliage in the interest of keeping salts from the leaves. The difference is that

If you have only one sprayer for all tasks, weed killer residues may kill your vegetables or ornamentals when you spray them for insects. Buy and use two sprayers.

salts in the irrigation water are harmful chemicals, whereas salts as fertilizers are plant nutrients. Nevertheless, do not exceed the stated dose. In other words, don't increase the amount just because it's good stuff you are using.

Spray during cool evening hours rather than during the mid-day heat. Stop spraying when you notice dark-green coloration to the leaves. There's nitrogen in houseplant food and you can easily give the plant too much. A strong color change is an unmistakable sign that you are overdoing it.

Even plants like strawberries can be watered and fertilized at the same time. It doesn't hurt to fertilize them while the fruit is developing—in fact it seems to help. And so we seem to be breaking our earlier rule—don't fertilize while the plant is developing fruit. However, strawberry fruits are not lightly attached to the plant.

Using a Hose Proportioner to Apply Sprays

A rubber tube attached to the side of this gadget is inserted into a gallon jug of water. A cupful of the appropriate fertilizer is added to the water in the jug. When the faucet is turned on, water passing through the hose draws the nutrient solution from the gallon jug to provide a solution equivalent to a tablespoon of fertilizer in a gallon of water—the original, standard strength.

When watering and feeding at the same time, it's important to use soluble fertilizers. Houseplant foods are usually soluble and are formulated to allow you to foliar feed. Read the product label to be sure. Sometimes houseplant food will contain urea—a useful and commonly used fertilizer—but it must be a pure form. Impure forms contain biuret, which is a harmful chemical when applied to foliage.

If you use a pressure sprayer to apply fertilizers to plants, remember to wash out the container with soapy water and rinse thoroughly several times after spraying. If there's any extra material in the tank, don't save it for next week's spraying. Fertilizers react with the metal of the tank and spray wand.

It's helpful to have two sprayers, one for foliar chemicals and another for weed chemicals. Label them—don't rely on your memory at a future date to tell you which one to use properly.

⚹ Pruning

Warm weather makes hedges grow again, so be quick to trim them before the vigorous growth becomes untidy. You don't want the plant to waste energy producing growth that you'll soon remove. Begin with light trimmings as soon as warm weather stimulates new shoots. Every cut you make encourages more growth, so you can thicken up a weak hedge by a series of light trimmings.

Straight-sided hedges require light, frequent clippings to be attractive. Informal hedges are best trimmed by taking the largest shoots, and following them back to their origin at the trunk and removing them there. The shorter "wild" branches can remain to maintain the desired natural, informal look.

A hedge that has become too wide and too untidy can be severely cut back this month. If you wait too long, the summer sun will scorch the inside branches that are no longer protected by the outer foliage. By letting in the light now, inside branches will send out new shoots and the smaller hedge will thicken up. An old hedge that has lost most of its lower leaves can be brought back by cutting everything off at a height of a foot or two. The stumps will quickly grow new leaves. If you wait until summer to do this, the strong sunshine will kill the newly exposed bark of the inner branches. The March sun will stimulate dormant buds to break out on the old branches.

Training and Thinning Grapes

There is often a lot of exciting growth on your grape arbor during late March that requires your attention. Thin out the extra crowded shoots by firmly snapping them at their base. Spread the remaining, more vigorous ones and pinch off their grasping tendrils to prevent them from hugging one another into a tight bundle. Train vines so they will cover your framework evenly. This also improves air circulation around plants, which helps reduce mildew infestations.

Pruning Frost-Damaged Plants

Many frost-tender plants begin to put out new shoots this month. As

Bacterial galls on oleander are unsightly and bad for the plants. Bacteria are spread by insects, rain and especially by pruning tools. The official recommendation is to carry a container filled with a solution of one part household bleach in nine parts of water. Dip the shears in the solution between cuts. Not many gardeners take the time to do this. A reasonably effective alternative is to spray the solution on plants after you complete the trimming job.

soon as buds break out into new green shoots, you will see the extent of last winter's damage. Cut out the unsightly dead wood plus two live buds in each cut; a cut into live wood encourages new growth.

Frost damage can be a definitive planting guide. If a lot of your landscape plants were killed by last winter's frost, with normal low temperatures, let it be a lesson to you. Replace them with plants that are hardy to cold.

✒ Pests and Problems

The spring season makes things grow, and "things" include more than plants. New leaf growth is tender and provides food for insects, particularly aphids. It seems we always have aphids in our gardens. During the winter it was grey aphids, largely feeding on plants of the cabbage family. Now the green, winged variety appears. You can also expect black aphids and yellow aphids to show up—all feeding on young tender growth. Squirt aphids with 50-50 solution of rubbing alcohol and water, or spray with Safers Soap®. If that doesn't work fast enough, spray with diazinon or malathion.

Young grape leaves are attacked by white flies and leaf hoppers. Leaves are full of sap and the surfaces haven't hardened, so insects find feeding easy and enjoyable. Later, their presence will be shown by lightly scarred silvery foliage. Quite possibly the insects will have dispersed by the time we notice the scarring.

If a cloud of little insects appears when you brush over the new shoots, you have a problem with leafhoppers or white flies. The treatment is to spray with diazinon or malathion. It's better to spray in the early morning or late in the evening to avoid the strong sunshine because the leaves are delicate.

Look in the strawberry patch. It's exciting to have the first flush of berries; most gardeners are keen to increase the crop by generous waterings. This provision of moisture, coupled with warming temperatures, is just right for snails and pill bugs, too.

Moist soil around plants simply invites them to become a pest. To stop them eating your fruit, you can pick them off—the snails, that is—and squash them. A cultural control measure is to water less frequently and allow the surface of the soil to dry out somewhat. Avoid using chemical controls on plants that are producing fruit that is ready to eat.

There's some controversy about leaf litter and its role in sheltering plant pests. One argument is that it acts as a surface mulch and keeps the soil cool and moist in hot weather. However, in this cool moisture there lurk pests and diseases. Privet weevil is a small beetle that spends summer days hiding. It comes out at night to nibble the privet leaves. Mildew of euonymus, roses and grapes are two additional hazards. Minimize these risks by raking up leaf litter around these plants. Compost the leaves if you like mulches, but discard the leaves of eucalyptus, Mexican palo verde and oleander. It's thought they contain poisons that harm plant growth.

Protect new growth on grapes, roses and euonymus from powdery mildew during March by spraying the young leaves with wettable sulphur once a week. Sulphur can burn tender new growth when it's hotter than 90F, so now is the time to start your control program.

Cut out destructive oleander gall every time you see it. The gall is a black crusty growth seen where the old flowers had bloomed. The bacteria that cause it hide in leaf litter. It's important to cut all the galls out. If you leave even a few, they will grow further into the plant and kill it. The bacteria that cause galls also can be spread on your pruning tools. The textbook recommendation is to dip tools in a can of 10 percent bleach before each cut. Send the diseased bits to the dump; don't leave them lying around to act as a reservoir of infestation.

Beneficial Insects: The Good Guys

There are good insects starting up their life cycle as a result of the spring weather. Lacewings seem to follow the population of leafhoppers. This is natural because leafhoppers comprise a large portion of the lacewing's diet. With their large, lacy wings, emerald green bodies and bright golden eyes, lacewings are clumsy flyers but beautiful friends of the gardener. Don't spray them—they can and do help you. Lacewings also feed on red spider mites—another pest of March. Ladybugs also eat red spider mites. More on ladybugs, following.

A word of caution: Don't get alarmed when you see an unfamiliar insect crawling over your plants in company with aphids, red spider mites, leafhoppers and whiteflies. This one will be a bit short of a 1/4-inch long, broad shouldered and tapering to a pointed tail end. It has the usual number of legs of all insects—six—but has no wings. It's body is mottled dull red and black or grey. At first sight it makes you

Flowers on fruit trees are obvious signs of spring growth. Insects do the pollination and you don't want to destroy them with sprays, even though the insect pest thrips can cause leaf twisting and fruit scarring at this time. To ensure a good crop, avoid spraying and accept the occasional, less-than-perfect appearance of foliage and the fruit.

March
In Your Garden

think of a miniature Gila monster. Don't spray this insect, either. It is the larval form of the ladybug. It's a growing kid and eating like crazy. Because it doesn't have any wings, it eats its way through the pests instead of flying away.

Adult ladybugs are notorious for flying away. In any case they are not particularly hungry when they are adult. It's a fallacy to think you can clean up your garden by releasing a pint of them into the garden. Yes, you can buy them through mail-order catalogs, and you can sometimes find a cluster of them in the wild.

Freshly hatched larvae would be a different story. However, with all biological pest controls we have to ask ourselves the question, "What happens to our friends after they have eaten all the pests?"

Praying mantises are another "good guy" insect. They usually appear a little later in the spring, but if you are watchful and know what to look for, you can bring them into your garden any time now.

Mantis egg cases come in two shapes, and they are plastered onto twigs of trees and shrugs. They can be seen easily while the trees are bare of leaves. There's a long case, looking rather like a miniature loaf of sliced bread. Each slice contains an egg—and there might be 50 of them. The other shape is an oval glob, tan in color, with the same sort of slight divisions showing.

Cut the twigs holding these cases and bring them into the vegetable garden, sticking them in the ground between your plants. It won't be long before they start hatching. If all the eggs hatch at once, the youngsters eat one another unless a slight breeze scatters them. They eat the first thing they see, so we hope it's aphids, red spider mites or leafhoppers—not their brothers and sisters.

Young praying mantises look much like little spiders. The adults are unmistakable with their front pair of legs held out in a praying attitude. Their nature, however, is one of preying. Keep one in the house near a window and watch them catch flies. Use a magnifying glass to give yourself a front seat to the original science-fiction movie.

Weeds

Keep after the weeds, especially if it rains. Those that germinated before Christmas are probably flowering by March, and flowers turn into seeds. Your first objective is to prevent flowering and seeding. After pulling or hoeing weeds, avoid the temptation to drop them on the ground. If the weed plants have formed seedheads, they go back into the soil and continue the cycle. Throw them in the trash.

March also is the time to use preemergent weed-killers. If it rains, or if you intend to regularly irrigate an area, get with it at once. These chemicals are not effective after seeds have germinated. Don't forget that preemergent weed-killing chemicals have no discrimination; they prevent all seeds—wildflowers and lawngrasses, too—from becoming plants. Don't expect "good" seed to grow in an area that has been recently treated. Because preemergent weed-killing chemicals don't affect established plants, you can safely spray the lawn against summer weeds. And you can keep the cactus patch clean for the summer without having to spend much time getting rid of weeds.

✓ Special Considerations

Cold Protection

March can have us worried about our flowering fruit trees. Some late varieties of peaches and apples could be flowering now, and so could some citrus.

Low temperatures merely delay flower opening. They won't hurt the trees. However, freezing nights are possible and you must be alert and ready for them. A freeze will kill flowers and a crop will be lost. It will also destroy recent new growth, which remains tender for a week or two after it has budded out.

On a freezing night, cover flowering fruit trees with a heavy sheet or light blanket. Better to be safe than sorry. If you ignore frost warnings, you might lose your crop, and it's a long wait until next spring. Remember to take off the covering in the morning and let the sunshine warm trees during the day.

A late frost is possible in March, so be ready to protect new growth on hedges and roses, flowers on citrus trees, and newly planted summer bedding annuals. All can be damaged by just one night of frost.

Inspect Plant Ties

When plants are growing vigorously because of warm spring weather, stems thicken as shoots lengthen, although it's not obvious. When you place ties on new growth, make them loose so the stems don't become strangled. Inspect all old ties and remove them if vines or trunks are squeezed.

Examine trees that were planted last month. You should have loosened the ties then, but new growth can be vigorous enough to tighten them again. When nursery ties squeeze a growing trunk against a stake, there's often an overgrowth at the top of the stake. If not attended to early on, the trunk will scar and the conducting vessels up and down the trunk can be damaged. It's a good practice to inspect plant ties all through the summer. For a good method of securing plants to stakes, see the photo on page 20.

March
In Your Garden

April

*W*hen *does spring arrive? We like to have calendar references, but this doesn't really help because every year is different—and there's no accounting for it. In the Midwest, gardeners put out tomatoes on Memorial Day because that's the start of spring there. But in the desert that's much too late.*

In our desert gardens, what signs should we look for? Over a general area there are the changes in day length. In other words, the mornings are lighter a little earlier. We may still be in bed and not notice this change. It's a lot easier to see that evenings stay light longer.

A week or two into spring you might notice that the sun rises a little farther to the north and, if you are truly observant, you'll find that one morning it rises due east and the same evening sets due west. If you looked at your watch on that particular day, there would be the same number of hours of darkness as daylight. You've passed the equinox—a true sign of spring.

Carolina jasmine is the first of our garden flowers to show itself in the spring. Newcomers liken it to forsythia, although it's a different family. Banksiae rose (Lady Banks' rose) comes next. Now it's the mulberry tree's turn. Before long a number of dormant plants are coming into leaf or flower.

Even so, spring has not arrived—it's probably a false start. Don't rush into gardening activity. Officially, there should be no more freezes after March 31 at intermediate elevations. But that's a statement from a statistician, and it's almost certain he was not a gardener. Experienced gardeners are waiting for warmer temperatures and welcome any reliable sign that they have come to stay.

❧ Featured Plants for April

Beautiful and delicate mesquite flowers appear when the weather warms up—but not on a particular date. The flowers are said to be a sign that temperatures will be frost-free. Summer is just around the corner.

Citrus

Within the tree, rising from the trunk of main branches, you sometimes will see fast-growing, straight shoots that come through the top of the tree. Some people call these shoots *watersprouts*. They usually remain unproductive and should be removed before they steal too much energy from fruit-bearing growth.

Another kind of unwanted growth is the *root sucker,* often growing at the base of the trunk. If allowed to grow, it may produce fruit that will be quite different compared to the rest of your tree. You will wonder what happened! Remove such sprouts, suckers and shoots while they are young.

Expect a lot of young fruit to drop off citrus trees after they have flowered, or even while trees are flowering. This is normal. Fruit trees produce far more flowers than they need to. It's nature's insurance against bad possibilities.

Newly set fruit is liable to fall off after a shock such as cold winds, a sudden hot day or two, allowing the tree to dry out too much between waterings, adding too much fertilizer or keeping the soil too wet. For now, those new fruits are lightly attached. Once they have become bigger than a thumbnail, they tend to hang on better. When they are as big as a golf ball, they are usually safe.

Most of last year's orange crop will have been harvested by now, but if a few fruit remain on the tree, don't get anxious—just pick them when you need something good to eat. Grapefruit will continue to improve in sweetness for another few weeks. It's normal if your tree is carrying old fruit, young fruit and flowers all at the same time.

Lemon trees are growing vigorously. Left alone, your tree will develop long, rangy shoots that consume energy and reduce the fruit-producing potential of the tree.

Walk around your lemon tree and nip out the tender growing points with your finger and thumbnails. This is called *soft pruning.* It checks forward growth and stimulates side buds to break out early. Side shoots produce fruit and they are the start of new branches.

Cucumbers

Cucumbers grow better in cool temperatures. Their immediate future is in question because it may get hot soon. Plants also need some shade and protection from wind. Cantaloupe, squash and watermelon like the summer heat and full sun, so their future is promising. Plant all you want, but keep in mind these plants require a lot of room and need plenty of water. Along with corn, they are not economical choices for the desert home gardener.

Prickly Pears

Prickly pears put on a gorgeous display of bright flowers this month. Annual wildflowers and perennials such as desert marigold and mallow also brighten the landscape. There are two kinds of buds on old prickly pear pads: flower buds and those that produce new pads. Now's your chance to keep a large prickly pear in check without hacking it to pieces, which seems to be the fate of many large old plants. Let the flower buds grow into flowers, but cut out the young pads; they

Grapevines are vigorous growers if given adequate water. The aggressiveness of the tendrils tells you that this plant is well supplied with water.

become *nopalitos,* which can be eaten as a pickled delicacy or sautéed. A small cut now saves a large portion of the plant's energy. It's a waste to allow a plant to grow too big and then chop it back.

Grapes

It's almost certain you are watering your grapevines well. Their springtime growth is so exciting that your natural reaction to the fresh greenery is to give the plant regular irrigations. And that's good!

The nitrogen fertilizer applied in January is now paying dividends and the growth is exuberant, to say the least. Forward tendrils that are longer than the new leaves, visible at the ends of new growth, are signs the plant is getting sufficient water. The tendrils are aggressively searching for something to wrap themselves around to support the plant in its journey to cover the trellis or arbor. (See photo, page 37.)

Sometimes these tendrils act so aggressively toward one another that you have to separate them. Go in now and unravel the knotted cluster of new shoots and space them out on the trellis. You can use soft string to fasten them to the wires. Make ties rather loose because the shoots will fatten up later in the summer. Some gardeners, after tying the vigorous shoots to the wires, pinch out the tendrils to prevent further aggression. This is especially useful to prevent new flower clusters being strangled.

While you are at it, rearrange the flower clusters so they hang free. It's a mistake to let them rest sideways between two shoots or squashed against a wall. If there's little room now, there will be even less as the clusters grow into bunches.

Below: Olive trees can be messy, dropping their ripe fruit during the summer. You can prevent this from happening if you kill the young flowers before they are pollinated by wind.

Below right: This picture shows the right stage for spraying—most of the flowers are freshly opened. Spraying too early when buds are closed doesn't work, nor does spraying older flowers that are pollinated.

It's an advantage to grow your grapes on an overhead arbor because the bunches hang down naturally—free and clear of obstructions. If they get caught up, it's easy for you to go in and release them.

If you think your grapevine is producing bunches too vigorously, go ahead and remove some of them. A first-year vine should produce no more than eight bunches; some experts recommend even less. Limiting fruit production allows the plant to develop its overall strength for future years.

If your grapes had mildew last year, you might need to spray the new shoots with wettable sulphur when they are 6 inches long. Spray every week until temperatures get over 90F. Sulphur becomes corrosive at such high temperatures. Spraying is preferred to dusting because you can get better coverage and it stays on the leaves longer.

Olives

Olive trees may continue to flower this month. To some people this is a blessing because they look forward to a bumper crop of olives in the fall. Others find it a nuisance because the pollen blows about and irritates them. Some homeowners don't like the messy fruit that are sure to follow the flowers in the fall. As we discussed in March, spraying a solution of plant hormone called Olive-Stop® will curtail fruit production. For complete details, see page 25.

Deciduous Fruit Trees

As a result of your pruning of deciduous fruit trees in January, there's a lot of new growth. Leaves have grown out of those single narrow buds and some have turned into new shoots. Good! That's next year's fruitful wood on the way. Even better, many of the fat, round buds opened up into flowers and most of those became small fruits. In some springs this doesn't happen to our liking. Bees weren't busy enough or the weather suddenly turned hot and killed the flowers. Winds might have chilled them or the tree became too dry.

But let's be optimistic and the tree is loaded with lots of small fruit on the branches. They might even be touching one another in clusters. It looks promising, so far. Now you must remove most of those young fruit! This is called *thinning* but what you are actually doing is *fattening* the remaining fruit. This is because most fruit trees develop many more young fruit than they can successfully carry to harvest.

It's normal for a heavily laden tree to cast off its surplus fruit later in the year when the stresses build up. Unfortunately, a tree might cast them all. Equally unfortunate, the tree might keep all its fruit—but they will be small. There's no telling. You have to rearrange things on the tree so you get a lot of large fruit. This task is more determination than skill. Commercial peach growers hire high-school boys to knock the surplus fruit off with long sticks. You should do it more carefully.

Take a look at the branches and try to imagine each little peach, apricot or plum at the size you like to buy in the supermarket. Now give it room to grow by removing all the adjacent fruit that would get in the way of it reaching that size. If you can't get up the courage to do the job, ask a neighbor over to do it for you. Don't hang around nervously watching him and making coughing noises. Go to his place and thin his fruit.

It's a tricky operation in some ways. If you don't take enough off, there'll be lots of little fruit at harvest time. If you take out too many, you'll get a light crop. If inclement weather follows, the tree might lose more fruit as a result of a sudden heat wave or a dry wind. Don't anticipate—do a good job.

Roses

You'll get more rose blooms if you harvest your flowers on long stems; try to get 18 inches of stem. With this method you are also pruning the plant lightly each time you harvest a bloom. A long stalk means cutting into a fairly thick stem and thick stems carry fat buds. If you pick your blooms with a short, thin stem, the small buds remaining on the plant will produce spindly shoots. As a result, your plant will remain weak in the years to come.

Strawberries

Continue watering strawberries for as long as they flower. You can help flowering and subsequent fruit production with a regular program of feeding as you water. Add 1 tablespoon of houseplant food to each gallon of water at every other irrigation—less frequently if leaves are dark green. If your strawberry bed is large, feed through a proportioner device attached between the faucet and hose. It automatically draws fertilizer through a tube inserted in a jug of nutrients.

Irrigate deeply to about 12 inches, and allow the soil surface to dry out between waterings. This procedure makes life uncomfortable for snails. The presence of snails tells us our garden and landscape areas are too wet. Constantly moist soil invites pill bugs and enables them to thrive. They are not insects but crustaceans. Pill bugs breathe through gills as do crabs, shrimp and lobsters. Their gills must be kept moist or they will die.

Strawberries might need shading now. If you are growing them beneath a grape arbor, there will be enough shade to keep the sun off the plants. As the sun gets hotter more grape leaves are produced—a nice arrangement. Strawberries in full sun will need shade this month. Erect a wooden frame or use the construction mesh wire from your winter tunnel garden. (See page 138.) Cover it with cheesecloth or shade cloth. White material throws off some heat and is preferred to the darker patio shade cloth. The covering also helps keep birds out of the bed.

Birds are not bright but they are persistent. If you cover your fruit before it is ripe, they can't find it—or so it seems. But if you try to protect your fruit after one or two birds have started to eat it, they will try their hardest to get through the netting or tear through paper bags.

Pecan Trees

Pecan trees have started their growth cycle. Warm-climate trees, they are usually late starters, although they require a moderate amount of winter chilling.

Follow the general rule concerning new growth: Water and feed trees. Pecans should have received a ground application of ammonium fertilizer in February, but pecans need more zinc than most other trees. Putting zinc sulphate in the ground is not an effective way to supply it to plants. Our alkaline soils "tie up" the chemical and plants are unable to absorb it.

Overcome this problem by spraying new foliage with a diluted solution of zinc sulphate—usually one tablespoon to 1 gallon of water. Spray once a week as long as fresh new leaves appear. It might require four or five sprayings. It's best to spray in the evening after the sun has lost its strength so the tender leaves are not burned.

These new, tender leaves are also the natural food of juice-sucking aphids. Pecans seem to attract aphids as much as roses. You can see them and you will notice they have left a shiny film on the leaves. Put Malathion 50® or diazinon in the zinc-sulphate solution and take care of two problems at once. Read the label for detailed instructions on mixing and applications for both.

Sweet Corn

Sweet corn sown several days ago should be doing well if the soil is rich. Corn is a hungry and thirsty plant. If it weren't so delicious, it would be considered a luxury in our gardens. To get good results with corn, give it all you've got. This means supplemental fertilizing every three weeks after it has reached 1 foot high, and until it starts to flower. Water all the time until you harvest it. Even if you prepared the ground well, corn will respond to side-dressing with ammonium sulphate. Scatter a cupful to every 10 plants and water it in well. Keep the plants green and growing.

We can't afford to spend so lavishly on a long-term crop. For this reason, sow seeds of short-season varieties. Besides, as with many summertime plants, flowering must be completed before hot weather settles in. Poor pollination leads to empty kernels—and heat is the usual reason for this.

Squash

Squash are good plants for children just getting started with gardening. The seeds are big and easy to handle, they germinate in warm soil in a few days, and plants produce an abundant harvest in little more than a month of growth. You can see them grow. There are many kinds of squash and you don't have to be particular about which variety to sow—they all do well. The favorites with most people are the zucchinis.

If you haven't tried the golden group of zucchinis, sow a few seeds for a pleasant surprise. The taste and texture are the same as green varieties, but the big advantage lies in the color of the fruit. Instead of searching through all that prickly leaf stuff looking to see if you have any green squash, the golden kinds are visible from a distance. It's easy to miss the green varieties, and if you do, it will turn into a giant before the weekend.

Zucchini squash are best eaten when they are small—just a day or two after the flower fades. Then they are tender and tasty. Harvest them regularly. The plant will respond by producing more abundantly. If you leave fruit to get bigger, the skin thickens, seeds develop and you lose gourmet quality. Old fruit needs to be cooked; young fruit can be eaten raw and enjoyed in salads.

Sow only a few seeds and two by two, not in a clump. Squash take up a lot of space and three plants are all you need.

If you want to eat squash all through the summer, plant seeds every six weeks or so. A good measure is to sow the next lot after you have picked three fruit from the previous sowing. You might want to break a gardening rule that says, "Once you find a good variety, stick with it—don't chop and change." If you sow only one kind of squash, you are likely to get tired of it by the end of the summer.

If you haven't grown butternut squash, give it a try—it's delicious. A lot of people miss out on this plant because it's called winter squash. They think it should be sown in the cooler time of the year. Not so—it's a summer grower, but you eat it in the winter. In other words it's a keeper and that makes it useful. In the hot, sunny desert it becomes a fine replacement for potatoes.

Sow butternut squash after the soil has thoroughly warmed up and there's no doubt summer has arrived. It's a sprawling plant and requires a lot of space, just like cantaloupe and watermelons. Grow it on a fence if you don't have ground space. The fruit are not too big, but you'll have to support them in slings as they enlarge and ripen on the fence. The newer bush varieties don't seem to be as suitable for desert conditions as the original vining kinds.

You can eat the young fruit, but most gardeners like to let them ripen on the vine and harvest late in the season, even after the vines begin to die back.

⚘ Planting

In olden times, European farmers judged the warmth of the soil by sitting on it—without the benefit of trousers—to determine when it was time to sow their fields with spring barley. The present state of the art allows you to test the temperature of your garden in a more accurate—and more comfortable—way. Poke a soil thermometer 3 inches deep in the soil in various parts of the garden. Take an average temperature. If the temperature is close to 60F, the time has come to plant and sow summer vegetables.

Be aware it can turn cold again and you may be surprised. Look around the garden for natural signs of warming soil. Harvester ants may have been activated out of their winter dormancy to start their year's busy foraging. Bee swarms tell us that spring is here and has come to stay. There are other signs, too, but they are less reliable. Bermudagrass lawns green up, mulberry trees flower, broccoli and lettuce bolt, and so on. There's a renewed activity around us.

There is one sign that you must observe with caution. If you notice a lot of fresh and healthy tomato plants in the nurseries, it doesn't necessarily mean spring has arrived. Years ago it was difficult to find tomato plants in the nurseries at the right time—early March. For some reason desert nurseries were still tuned in to Memorial Day as a kickoff for spring gardening, and that's too late. Now the pendulum has swung back too far. Some nurseries have a good supply of plants long before spring has truly arrived. Don't be misled by these early displays and plant too early. However, if you feel in your bones that spring has arrived early one year—and this does happen—go ahead and set out your plants. Gamble a little; take a chance! We know our seasons are short ones. By planting early, your goal is to get strong growth and fruit set on your plants before hot weather comes to stay.

If you misjudge the start of the spring season or a late frost hits the newly planted garden, you probably have to buy another set of plants and start over. There'll be time, and there'll be plants in the nurseries. What sort of advice is that—if it isn't contradictory? What *is* the right date for planting tomatoes, anyway? Nobody knows. Just watch the signs and do the best you can as early as possible.

Jump-Starting Summer Vegetables

What should you do when spring seems reluctant to appear, and the weather remains uncommonly cool? Gardeners are in a dilemma about planting warm-season vegetables such as tomatoes, eggplant and peppers. Plants have been available in the nurseries for weeks and they are usually in fine condition—inviting us to "go gardening."

A trick to jump start a growing season is to use a *starter solution*. Commercial starter solutions can be purchased at a nursery, or you can make your own. Put a tablespoon of ammonium phosphate in a gallon of water and shake well to dissolve it. Pour a pint of this solution into each planting hole—make lots of mud—prior to setting out your plants.

Some gardeners use vitamin B as a starter solution—it works. Others think phosphate is better because it's a nutrient. You probably have ammonium phosphate left over from soil preparation. Phosphorus encourages root growth and it's in short supply in most desert soils.

Easter Gift Plants

It's nice to receive azaleas and Easter lilies in the spring, but there are at least two reasons for not putting these plants in the ground. First, they have been grown in a greenhouse and rushed to flowering stage with chemicals that "forced" their growth. Second, they are not garden varieties. Even if they were outdoor landscape plants, they are not desert-adapted plants. They cannot tolerate the heat of July and August.

◖ Watering

Regular irrigation is important this time of the year. Continue to use the soil probe frequently (see page 69) to help determine when to irrigate. You must irrigate flowering trees, but do not apply fertilizer to them. Some gardeners get too anxious when hot weather comes on and overwater plants. Others become forgetful while they are busy with their vegetables—and their trees suffer. A warm, windy day can dry out plants quickly, catching anyone by surprise.

A sign that warm weather has arrived: the annual cleaning of evaporative coolers. The old pads may appear to be useful as a mulch to keep the soil from heating up, but do not use them in this way. They are full of last summer's salt, which will be watered into the soil and harm nearby plants. Throw old cooler pads away.

Recent Desert Plantings

Newly planted desert shrubs and trees should not be thought of as established arid-land plants—not yet. For a year, sometimes longer, water them as if they were rose bushes or mulberry trees. It won't be until their second or third year that they will manage on their own, and be "established."

Add Mulch to Conserve Moisture

We know that covering the soil on a hot day will cool it and retain moisture. Mulches of straw, compost and lawn clippings shade the soil and slow the evaporation of moisture.

So why not put the old cooler pads to use when we carry out our seasonal maintenance chore up on the roof? They are flat, wrapped in nylon mesh to keep everything together, and a suitable size. Unfortunately, they are impregnated with salts from last summer's evaporation on the roof. Don't use them. If you want, you can buy new ones for your garden!

Succulents seem to manage without a lot of watering, but try to remember whether they have had adequate rains to support spring growth. Use the soil probe to check for moisture. In April, a supporting irrigation may be necessary.

Native trees and shrubs may also need your help with irrigation if it hasn't rained. Older, well-established mesquites, acacias and palo verdes will flower on their own, but trees and shrubs less than two years old should receive a deep irrigation. Anything just planted in spring needs deep watering once a week; you want the roots to grow rapidly and as deep as possible.

Make your irrigation basins wider so the new roots at the ends of the branches continue to grow in moist soil. If you keep watering in a small, restricted circle around the tree, the roots will not move out into dry soil. A deep, wide-spreading, extensive root system has strength to withstand summer storms.

When you are extending the watering basins of trees, examine trunks that have been tied to stakes. In a good spring with favorable growing conditions, these ties can constrict the trunks as they fatten. Loosen the ties to anticipate this.

Fertilizing

Vegetables

If you are a new gardener or have started a garden in a new plot of soil, you may be disappointed with your plants' growth the first year or two. This can happen even if you took pains to prepare the soil properly. Don't expect to have an ideal soil all at once. It takes a few years for the organic materials you add to desert ground to mellow and blend properly. It will happen, but in its own sweet time.

Meanwhile, help your plants by providing them with nutrients as you water. Use 1 tablespoon of houseplant food in 1 gallon of water every time you irrigate. Those pale green leaves will turn to dark green. Don't overdo it with summer vegetables, which are largely fruit

Young tree growth can be encouraged by digging several holes around the tree as deeply as you can. Fill holes with organic matter and ammonium phosphate, and water out to that circle. When the roots reach these nutrient pits the tree will grow strongly.

bearing. If the foliage of tomatoes, cantaloupes, peppers and even corn becomes too lush, it can cause a reduction in flowering.

Landscape Plants

Some landscaping plants suffer from nutrient deficiencies that cannot easily be corrected by ground treatment. The answer is to "feed" young leaves as they come out of the bud. Young leaves have thin, delicate skins that can absorb liquid fertilizer. Before spraying, read the product label to be sure it's appropriate as a foliar spray. When the heat of the day has gone, thoroughly moisten the new leaves. Do this once a week as new leaves appear.

Insects—mostly bees—carry pollen from male flowers to female flowers, traveling up to a mile away. Insects don't stay on one plant when they are collecting nectar and pollen. They move from male flowers of one plant to female flowers of another, unwittingly cross-pollinating them. Because of this, never save seed from plants that have separate male and female flowers—even if you believe you have found a winner. Examples include corn, melons and squash. Seed will invariably be mixed and usually downgraded. Always buy fresh seed from a well-known seed company to ensure good quality.

You may get fruit that isn't quite up to standard. Sometimes it's downright bad. Often, it's because the parents of that seed became victims of circumstances beyond their control. It happens at even the most reputable seed companies.

Above: An instance of overzealous pruning that didn't help these agave plants.

Above right: Yuccas and agaves have a better appearance and require little maintenance if they are allowed to grow naturally.

Pruning

Mesquite trees weep black sap in the spring. All plants that go through a dormant period start up their cycles with a flow of sap; it's what makes the leaves come out. Sometimes, the pressure inside the plant is so great that the sap bursts out at a weak spot and forms a gummy deposit as it dries. When this happens to acacias in the deserts of Arabia, the result is called *gum copal, gum arabic* or *frankincense.* Admittedly, gumming can be a sign that something is wrong with the tree, but if it happens in the spring and lasts no more than a day or two, don't worry about it. If weeping occurs after you have cut a limb, the message is that you should not have made the cut! Cut limbs when a tree is dormant. Seal the cut with a spray of pruning paint.

Pests and Problems

Insects pollinate flowers of fruit and vegetables, so avoid getting too eager with chemical sprays during flowering season. Citrus thrips have a bad reputation but the scars they leave on the skin do not spoil the inside of the fruit. In an effort to spray them out, you are almost sure to kill a lot of other beneficial insects.

Blossom Drop

One of the troubles of early spring is that the nights remain cold even though the days may be warm. Summer vegetables don't like it because it slows their growth. If they are flowering, their pollen is not viable under these weather conditions. The flowers fall off so no fruit can form. It's bad news at a time when your hopes are high. But there's an easy way around this problem.

Hormone-in-a-bottle products are available at nurseries. Follow label directions and spray flowers when they are fully open. Although the material is labeled for tomatoes—it is called *tomato-bloom set* by some manufacturers—gardeners have also been pleased with the results on bell peppers and eggplant.

Saguaro Damage

If you see a black fluid dripping from a damaged saguaro, do something about it quickly. In fact, this stage may mean it's too late to save the saguaro. The bacterial rot that is causing the dripping will rapidly invade the soft tissues and kill the plant. To treat, scoop out the soft damaged tissue with an old spoon. Don't use a knife or you run the risk of inflicting further damage. As you remove the material, put it in a plastic bag and throw it away to avoid having the bacteria spread to other plants. Scoop until you come to fresh green tissue. Spray a 10% bleach solution (1 part bleach to 9 parts water) into the cavity once a day for three consecutive days. Leave the cavity open to air circulation. With time, it will scab over. Make sure rainwater will drain out of the wound; create a drainage passage if necessary.

Mildew

The warm weather induces new growth and new leaves invite mildew. Check for powdery mildew on euonymus hedges, roses and grapes. If you find it—it first shows itself as white blotches—spray with wettable sulphur.

Squash-Vine Borer

If you are fortunate to have your squash plants producing prolifically, bad luck may soon blemish this success story. And in this instance bad luck is called the *squash-vine borer.*

The first aphids of the year appear on oleanders. Aphids multiply quickly—females produce live young instead of laying eggs, and the young wait only a few days before they, in turn, produce live young. Expert opinions vary whether to leave these golden aphids or get rid of them, but you can easily kill them with a spray of the common shelf chemicals. If you take the "killer approach," start early before all new shoots are smothered.

April
In Your Garden

_____

_____

_____

_____

_____

_____

This is perhaps the most irritating pest in the whole universe of desert gardening. Squash seem easy to grow and it's so encouraging to start picking fruit only six weeks after sowing the seeds. Then one morning, you discover the plants are wilting and a good irrigation doesn't bring them back. You are puzzled and a little dismayed. A close inspection reveals a soggy mess on the side of the stem. Inside the stem there's a soft white grub about 1 inch long, eating its way along the stem and chewing up the conducting vessels of the plant—hence the wilt. The plant cannot tap into the moisture in the ground, and its large leaves transpire at a high rate in the summer sun.

This is a disaster of the first magnitude. The plant usually is finished just as it begins its usefulness. If you catch the problem early, you could try a little plant surgery. Slit the stem lengthwise, pry out the worm grub, dust with sulphur and replace the two surfaces of the stem. Bind together with a cotton bandage. Put a shovelful of soil over the repaired stem and water well. In most cases this treatment saves the plant and it continues to produce fruit.

Be aware that there's sometimes more than one grub in the damaged stem—make sure you find and kill them all. Old plants that have produced a lot of fruit and have lost their vigor don't seem to respond to treatment as well as young plants. Even after repair there's the likelihood that more eggs will be laid and new grubs will invade your plants.

Many gardeners try to avoid this pest by sowing seed about every six weeks. It is their belief that young, vigorous plants withstand an attack better than old ones. This isn't the case. Nor is it true that eggs are laid only on older horizontal vines and not on young upright stalks.

Whenever you see a quick-flying moth buzzing like a bee around your squash plants—expect trouble. This red-tailed, brownish insect is the adult, recently hatched out of the chrysalid stage. It spent the winter in the soil and you should have destroyed all of these chrysalides when you dug your ground in February. If they were not squash-vine borers, they were probably another pest that would cause problems.

Look on the sides of the stems for pinhead-size eggs—maybe five or six of them. They are the same color as the stem, but they stand out like little balls. Wipe them off.

Don't try to control this pest with chemical sprays. Because the squash plant produces both male and female flowers, insects are necessary to do the pollination for you. There's no point in covering your plants with cheesecloth to keep the pest out—you will be keeping the pollinators out, too.

Moths stay active through summer, so don't relax. Some summers, squash crops are a complete disaster because of this insect. Grubs attack all varieties so even butternut fruit is damaged. Fortunately, the moth leaves watermelon, cucumbers and cantaloupe plants alone.

✓ Special Considerations

Garden Cleanup

Clean out all the residues of winter gardening—if they haven't already turned to mulch. We unwisely keep many wintertime plants long past their real usefulness. Beets start to flower along with carrots, spinach and turnips. Sugar peas and garden peas develop mildew—yet we are reluctant to bite the bullet. They should go. They should have gone two weeks ago.

Protect Tomatoes When Spring Weather Gets Wild

The spring season in the desert can be a roller-coaster ride. Three or four weeks ago we might have had temperatures well over 90F, but last week we had hail! Gardeners who set out their tomatoes a few weeks ago and took care of them are smiling. Taking good care means keeping them out of the wind by setting up a shelter of clear plastic wrapped around a length of wire construction mesh. This, set around our plants, provides a sort of greenhouse to shield young plants from inclement weather. (See photo, page 26.)

Later in the year the plastic is removed and the plant grows in the "cage" created by the wire mesh. Plants grow up into the air to save ground space, yet produce profuse amounts of foliage and flowers.

Stake Trees

Newly planted trees should be staked against the wind. This will keep them from being blown over, of course, but the wind also does more insidious damage to newly planted trees, especially if the soil is kept too wet by a continuous drip irrigation system. The soil in the planting hole becomes well-lubricated mud; the tree's foliage acts as a sail and its trunk as a lever. As the wind causes the tree to sway in its muddy planting hole, new roots growing out of the planting ball into the surrounding soil are sheared off and broken. This means your tree will be slow in establishing. To stake trees, sink two stout poles into solid ground and pass soft cotton rope or other flexible material between them and the trunk at three places up and down the trunk.

Check Ties

Take another look at last year's support ties. Make sure they are loose enough so that branches grow without hindrance.

Install or Repair Lawns

If you haven't yet repaired your hybrid Bermudagrass lawn or planted a new lawn, now is the time to do it. Hybrid Bermudagrass does not produce viable seed, so you must plant sod or plugs, depending on your budget.

May

The elevation of your garden plays a primary role this month as to whether spring is over and summer is beginning. At cooler, higher-elevation regions, there's still time to plant trees and shrubs. They will establish themselves a lot more easily now than if you try to plant next month, after hot weather has arrived. Flowering winter annuals are still attractive enough to keep them a little longer. In lower-elevation regions, time has run out and winter color plants should be replaced with their summer cousins. No amount of deadheading will rejuvenate the pansies, stocks, poppies, snapdragons or others. Pull them up and replant.

The start of summer means the end of cooler weather, so we shouldn't spend any more effort with the remains of our carrot crop, or the onions, beets or lettuce left in the ground. Pull them out to make room to sow seed of squash, cantaloupe, watermelon, okra and black-eyed peas. All of these crops love the heat and grow vigorously, but they need a lot of water.

As water becomes more expensive, you might be forced to revise your concepts of certain crops. There's little point in spending time and money growing something you can get cheaper on the roadside or in a supermarket from mechanized agriculture. However, if you can grow vegetables out of season, enjoy more flavorful crops, or bring to the table gourmet vegetables that aren't available in the supermarket, it's well worthwhile. Additionally, there is the enjoyment you can get from overcoming the trials, tribulations and challenges of desert gardening. It's more satisfying than completing a difficult crossword puzzle. Everything you grow tastes better. Try it—you'll discover it really does.

❦ Featured Plants for May

Summer Flowers

This is the month for the "changing of the guard" in your flowerbeds. Cool-season annuals are feeling the heat and old age is affecting their appearance—replace them if you want color for the next few months. Pull out plants and inspect the roots for rots and deformities. Did the plants flower well, or poorly?

If your flowerbeds have featured the same kind of plants year after year, diseases may build up in the soil. Reduce this danger by planting different kinds of plants each year. You can also chemically treat the soil or use the solar sterilization process described on page 66.

Use steer manure, ammonium phosphate and sulphur to improve the soil, digging and mixing them deeply. Replant with annuals such as celosia, cosmos, impatiens, petunias, marigolds, lisianthus, verbena and zinnias. Most are available in nurseries. Avoid the temptation of buying leftover cool-season plants, even if the price is right.

Cactus

May is a cactus month, and you're sure to notice prickly pear bursting into flower. Look into the blossom centers and you'll see bees rolling in the scuppers like drunken sailors, overcome by the nectar. Now look up and see if there are any flowers on neighborhood saguaros; most likely there are. Now's the time to take photographs; the strikingly beautiful flowers won't last long.

The sculptural qualities of many cacti and succulents make them excellent low-maintenance accent plants. These agaves add interest to the landscape all year long.

Plant or transplant cacti now. These heat-loving desert plants recover best if moved during the month of May, before the temperatures soar too high. If detected, treat saguaro soft rot. To learn how to identify and treat, see page 47.

New pads on prickly pear that appear at the same time as the flowers are edible. You can buy them at gourmet food stores, ready to eat, or you can make your own *nopalitos*. Cut off the soft new pad and singe the spines over a flame. The skin will become loose so that you can remove it. Fry the slices or pickle them in vinegar with herbs of your own choosing; they make interesting eating.

Onions

After a long period of growing ever so slowly, you suddenly discover you have onions ready for harvest. Those varieties that are not adapted develop showy flowers. (The flowers steal nutrients from the bulbs and we get less to eat.)

As bulbs begin to fatten, scrape a little soil away from their tops each week and allow the sunshine to ripen them. As the stalks weaken at the neck and fall over, reduce watering frequency. Don't cut the stalks but let them dry out on their own. After the bulbs are exposed—sitting on top of the ground as it were—they can be twisted off at their roots and stored in a cool, airy place. They might keep for a month or two, depending on the weather, but not much longer. So eat them up with the outdoor barbecue meals our lovely weather allows us.

Garlic

Garlic and chives behave in much the same way as do onions. Set out seedlings in January. They are cared for in the same way as onions, too.

It's especially important to let garlic completely dry out before pulling them from the ground. If you reduce watering, the stalks will turn straw colored, but don't cut them. If there are flowers, bend the stalks over to stop the flow of nutrients reaching the seeds. The nutrients are needed in the *bulblets* or cloves. If you harvest garlic before the cloves have thoroughly dried, they won't keep. They should be hard and the pointed ends quite dry.

Roses

Roses need some tender loving care in May. They are at their peak at the beginning of the month but begin to show the effects of the heat at its end. Mulching is one of the best ways to provide comfort to your roses during hot spells. Mulches shade the soil and keep it cool, prevent moisture from evaporating, and keep weeds from growing. Although some mulches may provide a home for pill bugs, earwigs and crickets, the benefits outweigh the drawbacks.

Tomatoes

Tomatoes flower this month, but if nights remain cool, they may not pollinate. Gently tap the plant's stem with a little stick early in the morning while the flowers are fresh. The vibration shakes pollen from the anthers onto the nearby pistil. Another remedy is treating the flowers with a dose of tomato-bloom spray. Read and follow the precautions printed on the product label—don't use this chemical indiscriminately or your plants will suffer.

Squash

The first plantings of summer squash begin flowering now and give us reason to rejoice. But despite the lush leaves and numerous flowers, no fruit develops!

There are two reasons for this. The flowers you saw at first flush could have been all male flowers, which will never produce fruit. They look the same as female flowers until you examine the stalk behind the yellow petals. It's thin and long. Female flowers are borne on the same plant and have a short, fat fruit immediately behind them. Unfortunately, the first flowers are often males. It can take time for the females to appear. Once in a while the whole season passes and the plants simply won't produce female flowers—only males.

You can't do anything about it, although old wives' tales may recommend that you shake the plants, shout at them or pinch out the growing tips. Most gardeners, fearful of sideways glances from their neighbors, simply pull up the plants and start anew with fresh plants. Plenty of summer remains for two or three more successive sowings. Even if you have time to replant, it's no guarantee you'll have fruit. Pollination must take place.

Normally, bees, flies and ants move from one flower to another during the early morning hours when the squash flowers are open. Pollination is incidental to their search for nectar and pollen. The flowers drop off the next day no matter what happens. If pollination takes place, the fruit behind the female flower continues to grow and you harvest the result.

If the female flower was not pollinated, the fruit that is already fully

Below: Male flowers, identified by their slender stalks, will never produce fruit. They are needed for their pollen, which is usually carried to the female flower by insects.

Below right: This young squash, withering at the tip, is not diseased. It simply stopped developing because it was not pollinated in the flower.

formed, although small, turns yellow at the end, followed by browning and further shriveling. It looks just like a disease, which is what beginning gardeners think has happened to their plants, asking "What do I spray it with?" "What did we do wrong?" "What shall we do?" It takes a little time for them to accept the idea that poor pollination is the reason for their misfortune. "The fruit was there . . . now it's dying. The flower must have been pollinated." Well, it wasn't pollinated. To have fruit, pollination must happen. And sometimes you just have to do it yourself.

Early in the morning before breakfast, visit your squash patch and look around. Make sure both kinds of flowers are blooming—females with a small fat fruit behind them and males with their thin stalks. Pull a male flower from the plant and tear off the golden petals. You can eat them if you want—either fresh or fried in batter.

You have in your hand a stalk with a golden knob on the end, and there's a mass of sticky golden crumbs on it. Rub these crumbs onto the center of the female flower where there is a similar knob, only this knob is divided into three little horns. Voilà. You've done pollination, and it didn't hurt a bit. One male flower will pollinate four or five female flowers. (Do this every morning and you'll soon have a bumper crop of squash.)

Five days or so later, harvest the fruit. Wait until it grows to about 6 inches long. It's a mistake to wait for bigger fruit. First, bigger fruit get woody and develop seeds. Second, the more frequently you remove fruit, the more flowers the plant will produce. Don't sow more than three seeds at each successive sowing. You'll get all the squash you can eat—but only if you aid pollination.

After feeling pleased about successfully controlling the lives of your squash plants, you'd better take a close look at your grapevine. There may be a nasty surprise waiting for you. (See photos pages 58 and 59.)

This is a female flower with its fruit already started. This flower lasts only one morning and should be pollinated before it fades. If the insects don't do it, the fruit will abort. You'll have to transfer pollen from the male flower to its center to achieve pollination.

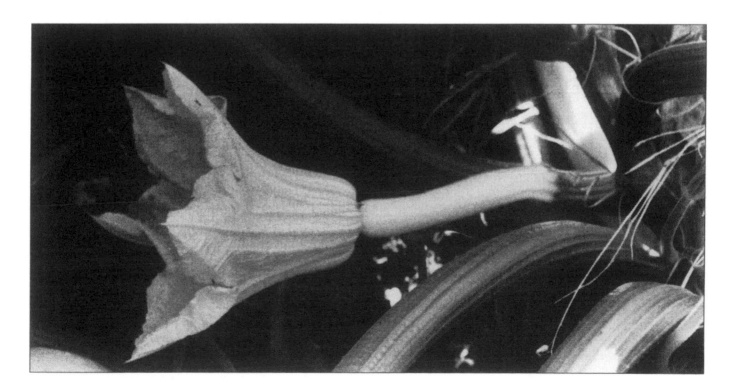

✿ Planting

Cantaloupe and Squash

Cantaloupe and squash like sun, so if you have spare ground, make a second sowing of these seeds now. They tolerate the summer heat well. You'll be able to sow a third and perhaps a fourth succession planting before cold weather comes on. They are greedy on space and water, so don't plant more than you need. A balanced selection would include three summer squash plants, four or five cantaloupe or watermelon, and four or five winter squash.

There are many kinds of summer squash. Seek out different varieties for each planting. This will give you some variety in your meals. Winter squash grow during the hot summer months. They store well so you eat them during winter. They are a desert substitute for potatoes. (It's not easy to grow keeper potatoes in the desert.) Winter squash have long vines and take up lots of space until frost arrives. Keep pinching out the leading shoots to stimulate side branches that will produce more flowers.

Cucumbers

Cucumbers are relatives of squash and cantaloupe, but they don't like the sunshine nearly as much. If you sowed seeds in March, you should be picking cucumbers any day now. It's too late for further plantings in May, but some gardeners take a gamble and sow the Armenian variety. For best results, grow them where plants will receive afternoon shade. Provide a tall trellis for the vigorous vine to climb. Slant the trellis at an angle rather than installing it upright. The fruit will then hang free and grow straight. Fruit grown in an upright trellis tend to get caught up and become misshapen.

Spinach Substitutes

Two other summertime vegetables are Malabar spinach and New Zealand spinach. Both can be sown anytime now. Neither is a true spinach, but you eat the leaves and they are a good substitute because they grow so well in the hot months. Simply pick a handful of leaves whenever you need a fresh salad or mess of greens. Picking keeps the plants compact and freshly branched. The plants can be grown in pots or in the ground. Malabar spinach, with its large glossy leaves, makes a dramatic plant in a hanging basket.

Sweet Corn

Corn is a hungry and thirsty plant. Water well and supply a tablespoon of ammonium sulphate to each plant every two weeks. Some gardeners worry about the basal suckers on corn plants. They consider them to be stealing nourishment from the main stem where the cobs are produced and pull them off before they grow too big. Other gardeners think of them as beneficial leaves that pull more energy from the sun and help produce a stronger plant—hence higher yields. It's the hybrid corn varieties that send out lots of suckers and, provided the soil is well supplied with nitrogen, there's no harm in them. Sometimes they produce a small, worthless cob.

Annual Color

Buy summer annuals that are on the point of flowering to be sure of getting the color you want; you can't rely on plant labels. A plant on the point of flowering is at the right stage to set out. Remember that close planting gives you more color per square foot more quickly. If you have a raw new yard, this is a good time to improve the soil. Your annuals will be glad you did.

Don't locate flowerbeds around desert trees. Flowering plants can grow well in the filtered shade of palo verdes, acacias and mesquites, but the irrigations the flowers need to keep healthy will be too much for the tree. Saguaros and prickly pear cactus are even less tolerant of ample water.

To make use of the shade these trees provide without putting their lives in jeopardy, consider growing your summer annuals in containers beneath them. Be aware that any container with a capacity of less then five gallons is going to be a nuisance when hot weather arrives—you'll have to water every day just to keep the plants alive. Daily watering keeps roots too wet and hot when temperatures hit 100F or more.

💧 Watering

When it comes to watering plants in the desert, it's not the "merry month of May." This month we notice it is getting hot and staying hot. The sun is higher and shadows are shorter. Days are longer, too—with the sun rising and setting more to the north. New parts of the garden are getting light.

It's time to be diligent about watering. Young fruit are on the trees. Apricots are almost ready and you shouldn't lose them to the weather or the birds. Apples and peaches are filling out nicely and they are vulnerable to hot, dry winds and rapid water loss. Newly planted trees are still establishing themselves and our summertime vegetables need a watchful eye. If they don't get a good watering, their first fruit will fall off and it will be some time before they start up again.

Good watering reduces the stress of 100F weather. Give first consideration to the newly planted things in your yard. Then irrigate the plants that are visibly growing, putting out new shoots. Next, irrigate everything else, even the cacti.

Fertilizing

It's a good rule to apply fertilizer to any plant when it is producing new growth, or is about to grow. Desert plants also benefit from fertilizer even though many have a reputation for thriving on poor soil.

A key to success is to apply small amounts of fertilizer frequently over the root area rather than a large amount at any one time near the trunk. Examine the plants around your landscape. Which plants are actively growing and which are producing pale green leaves? Those with pale leaves are showing a need for nutrients. It's possible the heat that will be present the next two or three months will cause them to go dormant and you should avoid fertilizing them at that time.

If you go by the calendar, May is a month to fertilize citrus. You may fertilize citrus trees in January, May and August, but there's nothing

Spring growth sometimes occurs at a rapid rate. It's wise to inspect plants often to make sure their growth is not pinched or squeezed. Plant ties should start off in a loose loop, but branches fatten as well as lengthen. Use soft string rather than pieces of wire to hold climbing plants to a framework. And keep an eye on them. See photo, page 20.

sacred about the timing. If the leaves are healthy and dark green, there's no need for fertilizer.

⚔ Pruning

Vigorous new growth calls for gentle pruning. Formal, straight-sided hedges of oleander, privet and boxwood may need to be tidied up by a light trimming. Don't trim oleanders if they are showing flower buds or you'll eliminate the spring color. Delay trimming until after flowering. Watch for vigorous growth on citrus trees, especially lemons. If unruly branches grow too long, the growth becomes too open and takes up too much room. Walk around the trees, pinching soft new growth between finger and thumb while the tips are tender.

While you're in a pruning mode, check the new growth spilling over hanging pots, especially those containing trailing African daisies, nasturtiums, hearts-and-flowers, periwinkle and verbena. Prune off long, straggly pieces. Use them as cuttings for new plants if you like, and you'll get new growth near the center of the plant. This encourages the plant to "bush up," which is what you want. Now's also the time to remove any frost-damaged twigs on shrubs and trees.

Support Branches of Fruit Trees

A heavy fruit crop can weigh down branches so much that they break. Did you thin the young fruit enough? To avoid serious damage, support this extra weight by propping up branches with boards. Grapefruit that hang in bunches near the ground can be placed on bricks or boards.

Take a look at the grapevines and sort out the developing bunches so they'll hang free of supports and structures. If you have had a very good berry set, you may want to pinch out the bottom third of the bunch and remove some of the crowded berries at its top where the stalk is. This will help produce bigger berries. Also continue to water regularly while the harvest is growing.

✐ Pests and Problems

You never knew there were so many pesky insects. But before you rush for the spray gun, consider that most bugs are not interested in your plants, some are beneficial and only a few are a nuisance.

Grape Leafhopper

This small creature appears in hundreds on grape leaves and rasps leaf surfaces to give them a grey or silvery appearance. Photosynthesis is interrupted by them even though the damage appears to be slight. As you walk under the arbor, you can hear them jumping off the leaves at your approach. Don't ignore them. They may appear small and insignificant, but a heavy infestation can rasp leaves so severely that they lose moisture and fall off the vine. The vine is trying to produce fruit, so replacing lost leaves is a strain on its resources. Spray with diazinon or Malathion 50®.

Beet Leafhopper

A relative, the beet leafhopper, is a more serious pest because it carries the virus that causes curly top, or leaf curl, in tomatoes. It feeds on desert plants. As these begin to dry out and die as summer approaches, it migrates to our green gardens, bringing the virus with it. There are so many of them and they come in waves, which makes it difficult to control them with sprays. You could enclose your tomato plants in cheesecloth to keep the tiny creature out. In the process, plants also benefit by some screening from the sun, but this will not guarantee complete protection. Planting away from afternoon sun does help because the leafhopper is a sun-loving insect. The best measure is to plant varieties resistant to curly top virus.

Orange Dog Caterpillar

The orange dog is a nasty-looking caterpillar that does a realistic masquerade as a bird dropping. It comes from an unlikely parent—the beautiful swallowtail butterfly. The caterpillars love citrus leaves and do a lot of damage before you notice them. Be observant and pick them off when you see them. You don't see tomato hornworms either until they have eaten a lot of your tomato leaves.

Cornstalk Borer

Early in May be on the alert for the corn-stalk borer. This is a caterpillar that lives in the stem and eats the folded young leaves. The leaves appear at the mouth of the plant in a ragged way—sometimes they are so eaten up they don't open out at all and merely lay over.

By the time you see the damage, it's usually too late to save the ear of corn. Try to prevent attacks by putting insecticide down the funnel of each plant when it is about 1 foot high. Dust and liquid forms are available. A dust stays at the mouth of the funnel and a liquid trickles down to the insides.

Chemicals to use are Sevin®, Malathion 50® or diazinon. One application should be sufficient, but if you discover that it's a bad year for stalk borers, make applications every 7 to 10 days. Read and follow the

Below left: Varieties of sweet corn with long leaves to the cob deter corn ear worm eggs from getting inside.

Below: Cobs with an open end invite the moth to lay her eggs close to their food. When the worms hatch they work their way down the cob and find food and protection from birds.

Above: It starts with this—the adult moth of the grape-leaf skeletonizer. It's a moth that flies in the daytime.

Above right: This slow-moving moth lays her eggs on the undersides of grape leaves. You have to turn the leaves to find them.

instructions on the product label. Too many gardeners have carelessly exceeded the recommended dose and burned the delicate tissue of the young corn leaves rolled up inside. If a strong solution gets on the growing point itself, the plant is finished—corn has only one bud.

If you don't like the idea of using chemicals, try Dipel® or Thuricide®—commercial names for *Bacillus thuringiensis,* a bacteria that causes terminal stomachache in caterpillars.

After you think you have taken care of the cornstalk borer, there's another problem waiting for you—corn earworm. This is the caterpillar you find inside the cob, eating the kernels. This caterpillar also comes from an egg laid by a moth. This time the eggs are laid at the mouth of the cob as the silks start to protrude. The caterpillars work their way down into the cob, under the enveloping leaves, where they are safe from birds.

Some corn varieties have a long set of protecting leaves at the mouth of the cob and, as a result, the pest is less of a nuisance. It simply can't get in. Varieties with open ends to the cob are very vulnerable. Once the damage has occurred, there's no point in worrying about it—you have to protect your harvest by anticipating it. As soon as the silks appear, apply three or four drops of mineral oil at the entrance to the cob. Eggs and young caterpillars will be smothered by the oil and the crop will be safe.

Pollination Problems with Corn

There's another cause of kernel loss and the most common in desert gardening. When temperatures reach 100F and above, it's too hot for reliable pollination. Pollen grains falling off the top flowers (tassels) take their chances that they'll reach the lower female flowers (silks). It's a perilous journey and they might be blown away by a strong wind.

Try "tapping" the pollen by putting a paper bag over the tassel before it puts out the pollen. It's less likely to be blown away if it starts its journey downward because of the bag. While there is no wind, gently tap the flower stalk to shake out the pollen. Should a pollen grain alight on the end of a silk filament, it still has a long way to go before it reaches the embryo—and often fails. Higher temperatures increase the rate of growth of a pollen tube and can exhaust it before it finishes its journey. High temperatures kill the life-force in the pollen just as boiling water kills a seed. It's too hot to sow any more corn seeds—wait until summer comes to an end.

Grape-Leaf Skeletonizer

If you have a grape arbor, keep a sharp watch for a 1-inch-long, blue-black moth that hatched during March. It's the adult of the grape-leaf skeletonizer, a most appropriate name. It's a daytime flier and easy to spot in the early morning when temperatures are cool, slowing its flight. It sits out on the sunny leaves to warm up. It's then that you catch it between finger and thumb. If there are a lot of them, you can catch a dozen at a time with a butterfly net. If you see two of them tied together by their tails, you can expect the eggs very soon. These are laid in clusters of 20 or more on the undersides of grape leaves. Before the end of the week they hatch into tiny caterpillars, which quickly turn into larger ones. Soon, their damage is evident in a few tattered leaves. If you ignore them, there'll be much more damage; whole branches will be skeletonized. By now the caterpillars are up to 1 inch long and have black and yellow bands around their bodies, like rugby jerseys. Control for this pest in its early stages is easy. Simply pick off a sluggish moth, pick off a leaf holding an egg cluster, or pick off any leaf that has a swarm of caterpillars on it. After the caterpillars have

Above left: The eggs hatch in a day or so to become caterpillars that skeletonize (eat) your leaves.

Above: Left untreated, your grape leaves soon look like this (and worse) after the skeletonizers are through! The plant is weakened and if you've been on vacation when these pests began their feast you'll be very disappointed.

munched their way over several leaves, you may have to spray with Sevin®, Malathion® or diazinon. Sometimes it's possible in the cool of an early morning to shake them off the arbor. They won't find their way off the ground back to the leaves. Don't relax. This is the first attack with others sure to follow.

Flea Beetles

Flea beetles converge on dichondra lawns in May. These small insects first show their presence by jumping off the leaves in clouds as you walk over the lawn, and then leave brown trails of damage on the leaves. A lot of them will exhaust a lawn. To control them, spray with diazinon or Malathion 50® on a calm evening after the heat has gone out of the sun.

Agave Snout-Nosed Weevil

These pests are active in May, too. You won't see the little black weevil until it's too late. It hides in the stems of agaves and yuccas, chewing away on the soft tissue until the plant can no longer absorb water from the soil, at which point it collapses. The infested plant is finished, but nearby plants should receive a preventive treatment as soon as possible. In fact, you might want to adopt a routine of treating all your agaves in May and again in September, when the beetles lay their eggs. Treat by pouring a diluted solution of malathion, Sevin® or diazinon on the top of the plant. Allow the solution to trickle down the leaves and into the heart of the plant and into the soil.

Weeds

Don't let summertime weeds get started. They begin as small seedlings and we tend to ignore them just because they are small. Many of them root along their stems as they spread and become a difficult nuisance. Summer rains later cause these weeds to grow at an alarming rate. A large garden quickly becomes a demoralizing place if you let weeds take over. A frequent light hoeing now takes care of weed seedlings and saves you trouble later.

A lot of winter weeds turn dry and brown in May, but that's not the

Euonymus is a common hedge plant that can be shaped readily, but is not a good choice for the desert. It won't tolerate exposure to full sun, and, when planted under the shade of a tree, it develops mildew, as shown here. Mildew can be controlled during the cool part of the year with wettable sulphur sprays (sulphur becomes corrosive at temperatures higher than 90F) but the damage scars the leaves. It's better to grow plants adapted to desert conditions.

end of them. If left to themselves, they will scatter their seeds. Gather the dying plants into bags before their seeds have dried and drop on the ground.

Bee Swarms

Bees are active in May, clustered on a tree limb or even at your front door. It used to be that bees were not dangerous and were more of a nuisance. But that was before our domestic bees were contaminated by Africanized bees (indiscriminate mating takes place in the air). There's a likelihood that new nests are a serious danger to you and your pets. Don't tie up your dog—its barking can antagonize Africanized bees. Also be aware that when you operate loud equipment such as lawn-mowers, blowers and chainsaws, you may become the target of their wrath.

Wild bees like to make their nests in places such as abandoned tires, boxes, plant pots and garden sheds. Don't poke around an established nest. Africanized bees are extremely and aggressively defensive. Don't get out the spray gun to blast the swarm with insecticides. Don't squirt them with water. In fact, don't go near them. The best advice is to call a professional service that has the knowledge and equipment to deal with bees. Look in the yellow pages under "B" to find the names of companies who remove swarms.

Powdery Mildew Disease

The standard treatment for powdery mildew on euonymus is a spray of wettable sulphur, but don't spray after temperatures reach 90F; it becomes corrosive in high heat. The fungus is supposed to die of the heat, but unfortunately, euonymus prefers shade, and so does mildew. Sunshine kills the mildew, but the plant can't take full sun either. This is a classic example of a plant that should not be used in the desert.

Cultural practices can reduce mildew attacks on euonymus. Observant gardeners say there's more mildew on hedges that have been systematically and frequently trimmed than on hedges allowed to grow more naturally. Trimmed hedges are tight and compact, becoming shaded by their own growth. Their density doesn't allow air to circulate and ventilate the foliage. These factors favor the growth of mildew.

Bird Pests

The tendency of birds to discover fruit and damage it before it's ripe is irritating. We spend a lot of time and energy—not to mention money—raising our own fruit and we have the right to enjoy it at its best. We should be able to leave fruit on the tree to sun ripen as long as possible, but the birds won't let us. There are some fanciful products on the market that are supposed to keep birds from eating your fruit, but not all are effective.

That original device, the scarecrow, is best made at home—though you can buy inflatable plastic ones. If you make it a family project, involving the kids, you'll at least get some fun out of the operation. Scarecrows, as well as stuffed owls, rubber snakes, children's toys, mirrors and shiny pie pans on a string usually work for only a few

May
In Your Garden

days—the birds simply get used to them. Changing their location makes them effective a little longer.

The latest idea is a silhouette of a hawk attached to a long pole with a piece of string. Birds don't like the appearance of hawks and this one's shadow moving over the ground, say the experts, is doubly effective as the sight of a hawk overhead. However, experience has shown that it's as effective as a stuffed teddy bear. Others have tried a large balloon, colored to look like a giant eye, left to hang in the branches.

Another item, somewhat costly if ordered through a catalog, is a metal face of a cat with marbles for eyes. It's suspended on a string and, as it turns in the breeze, light shining through the eyes is supposed to frighten birds. Birds even get used to interval bangers that go off every now and again like a cannon. If you try these, you'll frighten the neighbors more than birds.

Dogs are of little use, even if they are energetic and playful. But cats are very effective. The difficulty is to keep cats close enough to your trees to be a deterrent.

The only thing left is to cover the tree. Bird netting does work if used properly. You can buy it at nurseries in varying sizes, but it's likely that you will need to sew two or three together to cover the whole tree. It's necessary to wrap the entire tree; the net does little good just on top or halfway around. It's more effective to cover a tree completely with a sheet or a curtain material. This kind of covering hides the fruit from birds and bugs and protects it from sunburn. Enough light will reach the leaves inside. A sheet avoids the tangle of new growth that goes through a net and it doesn't ensnare cats or snakes.

If you choose netting, set up a plastic-pipe framework. For each tree, buy a fitting called a *cross,* and four, 10-foot-long plastic pipes. Fit, but don't glue the pipes into the cross. Set the free ends on sticks pushed in the soil to keep them from sliding about. Anchor the bottom of the net with bricks to stop the wind from lifting the netting or birds will sneak in.

To be most effective, the covering must be in place before the fruit interests birds. Once birds know there is fruit in a certain place they will not give up trying to get it. Half-eaten fruit puts out an attractive smell that brings more birds—and insects, too. It's nature's way of advertising a free meal. Dispose of all damaged fruit that is sending out these signals.

Some kind-hearted gardeners say that they don't mind the birds getting some of their fruit. Half for me and half for them, as the saying goes. Unfortunately, birds take half of each fruit! If they took only half of the harvest you might get by.

You don't need a net for every tree. Your "coverage kit" can move along with fruit harvests as they progress through the seasons. For example, once apricots are harvested, you can move the coverage to the peaches. Protect the earlier ones first and then cover the later varieties. Finish up with the apple crop. You can protect bunches of grapes and a very light crop on a young tree by tying a paper sandwich bag— not plastic—over each fruit or fruit cluster.

It used to be that the first ripe fruit seemed to escape the attention of birds, but this no longer appears to be true. It's also no longer true that birds ignore paper bags that hide grape bunches. Some seem to have learned that fruit is inside and they tear bags open.

Animal Pests

Rock squirrels go for apples in a big way. A net doesn't hold them back so you have to trap them. Box traps, baited with peanut butter mixed with oatmeal, catch them alive and you have to do the rest. It's humane in a way to take them far off and let them go, but this release of an extra animal in a balanced and potentially territorial environment can cause other problems, at least from the animal's point of view. Some gardeners throw the trap and its occupant into a barrel of water.

A tidy and perhaps more humane way to dispose of trapped animals is to put the trap, with its animal, in a plastic garbage bag and then introduce car exhaust fumes into it. Attach a length of flexible pipe to the exhaust and lead it into the bag.

Be alert to all of these possibilities in your garden. Don't relax a minute because if you do, there'll be a lot to cry about. As soon as you see something you know is damaging, take care of it. This means catching a grasshopper in the cool of the early morning when it is sluggish. Or tracking ants back to their nest and pouring insecticide down it. Or using a butterfly net to capture grape-leaf skeletonizer and squash-vine borer moths before they lay their eggs.

✓ Special Considerations

Take Care of Yourself

Work early in the day, but check plants in the afternoon. Temperatures commonly reach 100F and above during May, and outdoor work is best done in the early morning when it's cool. You feel comfortable and so do your plants. They don't show stress this time of day and it's easy to assume they are doing fine. But beware! Take another look at them at midafternoon. If plants show discomfort by wilting, irrigate and cover them with a white sheet for shade. Better yet, choose plants that can tolerate tough desert conditions.

The sun may feel nice but it is strong and damaging to your skin. If you plan to spend a lot of time outdoors during the next several months, take precautions. Gardening shouldn't be an accessory to skin cancer. You don't have to become a fashion model and buy trendy gardening clothes from a catalog. You will benefit from a wide-brimmed hat (not a baseball cap), a light-colored, long-sleeved shirt (not a tank top), long pants (not shorts), as well as gloves and shoes. Use sunblock on exposed skin. Drink water frequently while working, and come indoors when you begin to feel hot.

June

June is the month when we must begin our gardening chores early in the morning to avoid the daytime heat. If you're fortunate enough to have a grapefruit tree, it's stimulating to start the day with a drink of fresh grapefruit juice. Because the fruit is so ripe by June, it's possible to eat it like an orange—it peels and segments readily. Examine the thickness of the skin. It should be thin. If it is thick, let that remind you to reduce the amount of fertilizer you give your trees this year. The fruit is now getting past its prime and you need to harvest what remains before it gets puffy. In addition, young fruit from the spring flowering needs all the tree's resources.

An irrigation system is a good way to supply your lawn with the water it needs. However, the sunken sprinkler heads shown here require a lot of time-consuming maintenance. If the sod around them were removed, fresh soil added to fill the holes to the general level, and the sod replaced, a lot of mowing and trimming time would be saved. And the lawn would look better!

🌱 Featured Plants for June

Lawns

Grass lawns may show a characteristic dullness this month, followed by bluish green patches that turn into dead, straw-colored areas. Don't diagnose this as a fungus disease because it usually is not. Treatment for fungus invariably requires the application of an expensive chemical followed by a lot of relatively cheap water. The cure is effected by the latter, not the former!

Help your lawn survive June by mowing it a little on the high side, so the grass shades the soil. About 1-1/2 inches high is recommended for hybrid Bermudagrass.

Palm Trees

Hold off on pruning leaves and leaf stalks that clasp the trunk. Both provide shade that protect the palm's trunk.

Geraniums

Geraniums wither in the heat this month and begin to die back in July. Away from the desert they are perennial plants but they can't take our summer heat. Container-grown geraniums can be moved into the shade but those planted in a sunny exposure will suffer some loss. Some gardeners let geraniums take their chances. If the plants survive the summer, they cut them back to get fresh new growth in the cooler weather of September. If you try this, be warned that supplying them with too much water during summer's heat will rot their roots and the soil may become contaminated with bacteria and fungi, affecting future plantings. Geraniums are, to some extent, drought tolerant. It's better to water them lightly.

Tomato and Pepper Plants

High temperatures this month speed up seed germination but also cause gardening grief. Tomatoes, bell peppers, eggplant and cucumbers slow their flower production. Some varieties stop completely, although plants continue to grow vigorously. Those that continue to produce flowers don't set fruit because their pollen is killed by the heat. There are two remedies for this state of affairs. One, provide shade for the plants. Even if you drape light muslin or cheesecloth directly over the plant, you will lower temperatures and reduce the sun's intensity. You will also trap humidity around the plant, and this appears to be beneficial.

The second solution is to spray the flowers with tomato-bloom hormone. Read the instructions on the bottle before spraying (don't spray too many times). The hormone stimulates fruit development without pollination. As a side benefit, the resulting fruit have few seeds.

Experienced gardeners also select suitable varieties to overcome this summer problem. Cherry-type tomatoes accept the heat and will produce fruit continuously, but not everyone likes a summer full of cherry tomatoes. Plant breeders are developing bigger-fruited kinds of cherry tomatoes so the future looks promising. Meanwhile, don't try growing Beefsteak or Super Beefsteak varieties. They are just not adapted to the desert and you're almost sure to be disappointed with low yields in spite of large, leafy plants.

Grapes

Early grapes are ripening—enough to make the fruit interesting to moisture-seeking birds. The bunches aren't ready for us just yet, but birds work fast. If you don't bag them now, there won't be anything for you next month. Use brown paper sandwich bags and staple them closed up at the top end of the bunch. There's no need to punch air holes—that will merely provide openings for birds who will tear the holes larger. Don't use plastic bags because they will cause the fruit to spoil.

While you are putting paper bags on the bunches of ripening grapes to protect your harvest from birds, take a look at the ties used to train vines in the spring. Let's hope you did not use paper-covered wire. These are easy to use and look innocent enough with their soft covering, but they don't stretch. They might be so tight they are cutting into the shoot. Be aware that nylon string doesn't stretch nor does cotton string. Take a careful look at all of last spring's ties and loosen them. Some may have to be cut.

On the left the grass is good, although perhaps a little on the long side. Mowing it too closely can lead to sun scald. The lesson is to avoid allowing the grass to get too long and then removing it all at once. Take two mowings to get to the recommended height.

The soft, green plastic ribbon (it comes on a roll) is a suitable tie material because it stretches. Thin kinds are available for small, soft plants and a thicker version is preferred for trees. Use the thin material for grapes.

New shoots will continue to develop during the summer and you should regularly guide these and tie them. Avoid a cluster of new shoots entangling themselves with their searching end tendrils.

↓ Soil Preparation

Sterilizing the Soil

The soil reaches its warmest temperatures during July and August. We can benefit from this by using the sun to sterilize soil contaminated with nematodes and weeds, especially troublesome nutgrass. Let's call it *summer fallowing*. Ordinarily, chemicals are expensive, dangerous and not completely effective in controlling weed seeds, Bermudagrass, nutgrass, fungus diseases and insect grubs. Sun-powered soil sterilization is cheap, effective and harmless to the environment. Of course, you'll have to stop using your garden for a while, but if it's been in decline because of a buildup of pests over the years, this month is your opportunity to tackle the problem.

Begin the process as soon as June temperatures go above 100F and are likely to remain there as the daily high. Clear out all dead plants and pull weeds. Turn on the sprinkler to moisten the soil down to 18 inches. Cover the area with a sheet of clear plastic and secure in place with bricks or stones on the edges. This keeps the wind from blowing the plastic back and opening up the area to dryness. Let the sun cook everything under it. At first some weeds will germinate and established weeds will grow rapidly. But it won't be long before the heat becomes too much and they die. The same thing happens to soil organisms— both the good and the bad. If your soil has an excess of bad ones such as nematodes, snails, pill bugs, fusarium wilt, verticillium wilt and so on, the operation is worth it.

Leave the plastic in place for one month. After the month has passed, remove the plastic and dig the ground to bring the lower layers

The summer season gives gardeners a chance to sterilize the soil by sunlight. Fungi and bacteria can be killed by solar heat trapped under a sheet of clear plastic. First wet the soil then cover it with clear plastic for a month. Next, dig the soil to expose the lower layers, wet it and cover it again for another month. See text for complete instructions.

of infested soil to the surface. Wet down the area and replace the plastic for one more month of solar cooking.

Solar sterilization is an effective way to sterilize the soil that doesn't pollute the environment. Plus you can plant as soon as you remove the plastic.

Planting

Security Plantings

June is a good month to install a security barrier of heat-loving cholla and prickly pear. These are excellent plants to keep out stray dogs and trespassers. They also discourage graffiti artists from vandalizing your wall or fence. To plant, loosen the soil, partially cover various-size pieces of the pads or segments, water in and walk away. New roots will grow and plants will establish quickly.,

Sow Seeds

There's a lot of exuberant growth during June. Sow seeds of squash, melons, okra, black-eyed peas, amaranth and yard-long beans. (See following.) All of these love the heat and their seedlings pop out of the soil in three or four days. It's satisfying for new gardeners or kids.

Yard-Long Beans

Yard-long beans make a wonderful summertime crop, thriving in the heat and sunshine. They produce an abundance of long green beans through the summer, until they are killed by frost in November. There are a number of varieties that go by names other than yard-long beans, depending on the catalog. Look for asparagus beans or Chinese pole beans. The "pole" part of the name tells you that you should provide a trellis. Make it more than 6 feet high and don't set it upright, but slant it at a slight angle. The beans hang straight, making them easy to pick.

And pick you must. Yard-long beans grow vigorously and produce abundantly. The pods are best gathered before they harden into a string of beads. This calls for picking twice a week. You can let the seeds dry on the vine and harvest hard beans, but that's not the point. In summer, chop the tender beans for fresh salads. If you steam the long pods, do so only lightly so they simulate asparagus. You won't need a large acreage of this crop. A 10-foot row with plants 12 inches apart trained up an 8-foot framework will keep you and your family well supplied all summer.

One gardener lost sight of his mobile home after planting a row of seeds on its sunny side. It turned into a heap of greenery. He couldn't eat all the beans. Many of them ripened and fell to the ground. The next summer he had to hack his way to the front door. He had a habit of wandering with his friends but he never got lost; it was easy to find home. It was the biggest mound of vegetation for miles around in the hot, dry, brown desert!

Squash—Time to Pollinate

Early morning is the time to carry out a daily chore on your squash plants—hand pollination. Sometimes the bees give your garden a wide berth and the smaller insects don't do their stuff, either. See step-by-step instructions, page 52.

💧 Watering

June is the month when our water bills increase. If your landscape plants don't get the water they need, they will tell you. A dry lawn looks dull and bluish, turns silvery, then turns a straw color. Privet and roses wilt and develop brown sunburn patches on their leaves. Yellow leaves are common inside the canopies of trees, and new growth has a dull rather than shiny appearance. If the drought continues, trees drop the yellow leaves; *Rhus lancea,* African sumac, is a notable example. Pine trees drop needles as well. Citrus fruit might drop young fruit due to the double stress of increasing temperatures and inadequate water.

Avoid trouble by paying attention to your plants' water requirements. You'll have to water more often that you did in May, but don't make the mistake of watering too often, such as every evening, with a light sprinkling. This only moistens the top inch or two of soil.

Deep Watering Is the Rule

Deep water all your plants this month. This means getting a reserve of moisture in the soil that will last a long time. It also means encouraging roots to grow deeply to follow this moisture, moving away from the high temperatures near the soil surface. An example of this can be seen by observing tomato growth. A sprawling tomato plant shades the soil with its foliage. It produces fruit longer into the summer than one that's been staked up so that the sun bakes the soil around it.

Deep watering is always wise, but especially beneficial to trees and vines that were planted in January. Their roots are just getting out of the planting ball and will die soon after contacting hot, dry soil. Forgetting to irrigate causes these newly planted plants to lose the momentum of spring growth. If it's an unusually hot June there's a danger new growth will die back. Such a setback might result in causing fruit-producing trees to need another entire year before the first crop.

Don't sprinkle the foliage of any plant believing you are helping cool it down. Desert landscape plants can tolerate dry heat. Other "less tough" plants don't like the salts that form on their leaves after the water evaporates.

Newly installed sod should be watered regularly until new growth fills in the edges. Once the edges dry, the grass dies and you'll have a patchwork instead of a smooth green lawn. This is especially true on a slope. Water doesn't soak in but runs off.

The opportunity may arise to reuse water from your bath, clothes washer and swimming pool. Provided that there's not a lot of sodium in these waters—from soaps in baths and clothes washers, and as residue from chlorine powder from pool water—you can turn the outflows onto ornamental plants and lawns once in a while. The high-quality tap water can be reserved for vegetables and fruit trees. Your Cooperative Extension office will have a list of detergent soaps that are safe to use on the soils common to your area.

How to Irrigate Trees and Shrubs

Make a shallow basin around the plant a little beyond the *drip line,* an imaginary area where rainwater drips off the outside perimeter of the plant's foliage. A plant's feeder roots are located at the ends of main roots—just like leaf shoots are found at the ends of branches. This is why watering next to the trunk does little good. For a large tree such as pecan, the lip of this basin may be 6 inches high. For a small shrub it may be a few inches high.

Fill the basin with water, then turn down the faucet so the water is absorbed by the soil at the same rate. Keep this "head of water" until you can easily push your soil probe into the moistened soil 2 feet deep for shrubs, 3 feet deep for trees. Depending on soil type, this may take three hours of watering—longer for slow-draining clay soils.

As plants grow, extend their watering basins. If your landscape has sloping ground, channel rainfall runoff to your plants. Leave basins that might receive runoff open on the high side to collect the water.

After deep irrigating established trees, it's safe to wait until the top few inches dry out before watering again. How long this will take depends on many factors: soil type, exposure to wind and sun, plant size and type and time of year. Check the soil yourself to be sure.

When? How Often?

Gardeners ask themselves and one another a good question at this change of season: "What's the best time of day to irrigate—morning or evening?" If you irrigate in the evening, the plants have already gone

Below left: As a tree grows, it needs a wider watering. This "well" should not be dug deeply, but the soil should be shaped to form a berm that holds the water as far out as the drip line (See photo, page 28.)

Below: As the weather warms there's a greater need to monitor how much water is in the soil. Your soil probe becomes a valuable tool to tell you if the soil is wet or dry, and how far down moisture has reached. It won't penetrate dry soil, but slides easily through moist soil.

through a bad day and you merely pull them back into a good state. Their wilt disappears and they look good again. On the other hand, if you water in the morning before it gets hot and stressful, your plants are more prepared to take the strain of midday heat. This argument is particularly true if you make the mistake of sprinkling the soil lightly instead of giving it that good, deep soak that lasts six or seven days.

Don't confuse dieback of twigs caused by cicadas damage with that caused by drought. They look similar and appear at the same time—stressful, high-temperature period before summer rains.

Continue to check the soil's moisture content at root depth with your soil probe. This tool is your best friend in June. Water deeply when you irrigate so moisture reaches the root area. Avoid the temptation to lightly sprinkle plants when you get home from a hot, tiring day.

Saving Water

There are many ways to save water. First, a deep soak uses water efficiently, putting it where it is needed, promoting deep roots. Water won't evaporate if it is deep down in the soil. Second, conserve water by covering the soil with a straw or hay mulch. Third, don't sprinkle or use sprinklers that throw water high into the dry air. A portion of it evaporates before it falls to the ground. Fourth, when possible, shade plants to keep them cool, which slows their metabolism.

Hoses and Hot Water

If you leave a garden hose out in the sun, don't forget it is full of hot water. Don't apply to your plants, but onto the compost pile or around an established tree. Follow with cool water to reduce soil temperature.

Summer Mulches

A mulch is any material laid on the ground around plants to modify adverse conditions. A mulch insulates the soil from the hot sun and drying winds and suppresses water-stealing weeds. Mulches can be made from old carpet, unfinished compost, new cooler pads (used ones contain too much salt), newspaper, tree bark, forest products and bagged "mulches" available from nurseries.

Within reason, the thicker the better (up to 6 inches), but a lesser amount is better than none. Thicker mulches are better at suppressing weed growth. Mulches have little nutrient value but as they decompose they add valuable organic material to the soil.

Mulches are largely beneficial but they do have some negatives. First, an extremely thick mulch will keep water from a gentle rain or light irrigation from reaching the soil, absorbing moisture like blotting paper. Second, desert winds can blow mulches around, making the landscape untidy. Third, thick mulches can provide a cool and moist hiding place for pill bugs, crickets and other insects. (They repay your hospitality by eating your plants.) Fourth, a winter mulch prevents the sun from warming the soil.

Fertilizing

June is not a typical month to fertilize. Your fall soil preparation continues to provide dividends. However, trees and shrubs that were planted last year may need a boost of nutrients now that they have become established. If leaves are pale and small, apply a small amount of ammonium sulfate. Use a tablespoon for each gallon of water and sprinkle widely around the plant -but not against the trunk. Do this about once a month.

If you have been mowing your Bermudagrass lawn frequently because it has been growing vigorously in the warm weather, apply 1 pound of ammonium sulfate for every 100 square feet and water it well to keep the grass green and growing.

Pruning

If you have formal clipped hedges, perhaps they've lost their neat shape. It's time for a gentle trim. Informal "wild" hedges don't show their growth until they block the driveway or sidewalk. Find the foremost branch and follow it back to its origin. Cut it off flush at the main branch. If it is thicker than your thumb, seal the ends with a spray of pruning paint. During these hot days, open cuts dry out and peel back,

Remove the straggly top of hedge plants to get the hedge to thicken up with new shoots down below.

exposing the wound and allowing easier entry of pests and diseases.

If you want your newly planted shade trees to have a tall canopy you can begin removing the bottom two or three branches. It's best to do this gradually—about every 10 weeks—to aviod sunburn onthe trunk.

Pests and Problems

June is a buggy month. You can blame the increase in humidity, but the monster insect of the desert hasn't appeared yet. It needs heavy drumming of raindrops on the soil to make it change from a 3-inch fat grub into an adult, giant, whirring beetle that scares old ladies and little children out of their wits. More on this creature on page 81.

Search for Squash-Vine Borer Eggs

Time to inspect the stems of squash plants for eggs of the squash-vine borer. They are laid two or three at a time on the outside of the stem. They are about the size of a pin head and can easily be rubbed off. If they remain, you have a much bigger task later on after they hatch and burrow into stems and eat up the insides. An ounce of prevention is worth a pound of cure. Consider this a daily task.

Beet Leafhoppers—Again

As mentioned last month, in years of ample rains when desert growth is luxurious, there is an accompanying large population of insects. When the annual weeds and flowers dry out and die, these insects migrate to the next conveniently located green patch—our summer vegetable gardens. One particular insect, the beet leafhopper, brings curly-top virus with it. Signs of this incurable disease begin to show just as we start to pick the first tomatoes. An infected plant shows wilted, stunted growth and poor flowering. Often, these plants die, but occasionally they throw off the disease, struggle through the stresses of summer and revive to give us a fall harvest.

Plants in full sun are more attractive to the beet leafhopper than

Cicadas spend most of their life in the soil as grubs, chewing on bits of vegetation. During the summer rains, they leave the soil, climb upwards, discard their body cases (shown here) and fly away. As grubs they are not a serious danger, but the adult female lays her eggs in a series of notches on tender shoots. The end leaves die and you think something is wrong with the tree. The damage is minor, however.

those that are shaded—for even part of the day. This suggests that shading offers some protection, but you will keep the pest out completely if you build a wire cage and surround your tomatoes with cheesecloth. Up goes the price of tomatoes! If you take your chances, you could have a complete disaster. Dead plants are a source of infection, but the soil can be used again when the danger has gone. Dead plants can be composted.

Leaf-Footed Plant Bug

The leaf-footed plant bug makes its appearance in June. It's aptly named because its hind legs have flattened sections that look like small leaves. The front end—its snout—is the nasty part. The bug feeds by sucking plant juices through its long piercing snout. In the process it introduces bacteria. These bacteria cause rot spots or, in severe cases, completely destroy the fruit. Favorite plants include pomegranates, tomatoes and nuts such as pecan.

Cicadas

An unmistakable herald of approaching summer rains is the cicada. More correctly, we should speak of them in the plural because there's no such thing as one cicada. They sound off as if there are hundreds. "I've never seen anything like them" is the common cry. People must have short memories!

Cicadas live most of their lives in the ground as grubs, similar in appearance to the June beetle grubs we turn up when digging the vegetable bed. In the Midwest they are called seven-year locusts, but that's an inaccurate name in both aspects. It's not known exactly how long they stay in desert soils, but they come out in scores every June and climb upwards. You see their skeletons sticking to tree trunks, walls and even the front door. (See photo, opposite.) The split back tells you the live part has gone on, and your ears tell you that they are all over the place. It's the male sending out sexual signals to lure females to a tryst, after which eggs are laid.

It's the egg laying that does some damage to our trees—either ornamental or fruit trees. The female cicada makes a number of little incisions on tender twigs and lays an egg in each. The result is the sawtooth appearance of the terminal twigs, which often die back. It's a sort of gentle pruning and doesn't usually do a lot of damage to a tree, although it does leave plants looking scorched at the edges. The eggs hatch and grubs fall to the ground. The grubs spend the next year or so eating decaying organic material, but they also attack the roots of living plants.

Chemical controls are not worthwhile because cicadas don't stay in one place for long. They are 20 times the size of a housefly and a lot of poison is required to overcome their hard protective exterior. There's little point in spraying the ends of tree growth. The spray evaporates quickly in the hot air and leaves little residue.

A species of wasp is a natural predator of cicadas. It is appropriately called *cicada killer wasp*. It's the largest wasp in the desert and is capable of stinging the cicada as it flies around. The cicada body is brought to a hole in the ground and stuffed in to provide food for the baby wasps.

June
In Your Garden

Wasps are high on the list of beneficial insects—as long as you don't get stung by them. They eat aphids, mealybugs, red spider mites and other small insects that cause a nuisance to our plants.

Combat Heat Stress

In the dog days before summer rains make their appearance in July, the heat is oppressive. It's common for temperatures in the shade to reach 105F and more. The sun is fierce and there are plenty of indications that plants are suffering; one obvious sign is wilting at the ends of new growth. Grapes provide a good example of this. Other signs are when leaves drop off fruit trees and vegetables such as bell peppers and eggplant.

A most common sign of heat stress is a dull, yellow patch in the center of a leaf. Sometimes this patch turns white and dead, right in its middle. It is common on citrus leaves but appears on other trees that have glossy leaves. You'll sometimes find the same dead patch on ripening bell pepper and eggplant fruit. This is sunburn, and it becomes worse if you let your plants go a day or two without watering. Be attentive.

Shade cloth is of value this month. The dark material should be attached to a tall framework so air moves over the plants easily. White shade cloth can be placed closer to the plants—even directly on them—because it reflects a lot of heat in addition to providing shade.

If you erect a permanent shade structure, keep the angle of the setting sun in mind; the afternoon sun may shine below the shadecloth. The west end of your garden will be exposed to hot sun for a few hours unless you extend the shade area 3 to 4 feet beyond plantings or allow the material to hang down 2 or 3 feet, much like a table cloth. Make a scale model on a board and set it out in your garden to determine sun-and-shade patterns before cutting cloth and erecting frames.

It is not necessary to shade corn, squash, any of the melons, black-eyed peas, Chinese pole bean or okra. All of these enjoy the sunshine.

If peaches or apples are hanging at the ends of branches, consider placing shade cloth over the trees. Protect bunches of grapes from the sun and birds by slipping a paper sandwich bag over the bunch and stapling it at the top. There's no need to make breathing holes—the grapes are safe in the bag.

Citrus trees and their fruit tolerate the heat and sunshine as long as they are well supplied with moisture. Once the young fruit have reached golf-ball size there should be little fruit drop, but don't be complacent. Watch the soil moisture and let the soil probe tell you when it's time to irrigate.

Stressed Tomatoes and Blossom End Rot

Fruit rot may appear on tomatoes now that the weather is getting hot. It's hard for gardeners to accept and understand this malady. They ask, "What have I done wrong?" The ripening fruit shows a dark, corky, shriveled patch at the flower end of the fruit. You can cut this piece out and eat the fruit. You'll probably be tempted to do this because this is the start of your harvest and you are naturally eager to get something back for your patient, hard work during a difficult spring.

Blossom end rot, plant physiologists tell us, is not a disease, but a "condition." It is caused by stresses within the plant, not by a fungus or bacteria, even though the appearance strongly suggests it. The stresses are caused largely by improper watering and high temperatures. Heat affects calcium uptake by the plant. Constantly wet soil means low oxygen for root function—and that creates stress. Undoubtedly, bright intense sunshine and the general unkindness of June weather in the desert also have something to do with it.

The fruit's condition doesn't improve with time. If you have a lot of green tomatoes with a black end, you might as well pull them off and let the plant try again. Don't water so much that the soil remains too wet and don't let it become too dry, either. Let the water soak slowly into the soil. Shading plants may help reduce stress and cut back on the blossom end rot problem.

✓ Special Considerations

Harvesting Eggplant and Corn

How do you know when to harvest eggplant and corn? There's a tendency to let eggplant stay on the plant too long in the hope that you'll harvest a fruit as big as those you buy in the stores. Ignore size as a guide and watch the shiny bloom on the fruit. As soon as the shine turns dull, the fruit is getting old. The seeds inside begin to harden and the flesh gets rubbery. The kinds that do well in the desert are the small-fruited ones—Japanese varieties.

To help ensure you'll get a good cob of corn, make a daily inspection soon after the silks turn brown and dry. Peel back a little of the enveloping sheath to expose the kernels. If they are plump and moist, the cobs are ready for boiling water. If the kernels are skinny, replace the sheath leaves and secure them with a rubber band. Look again in a couple days, remembering corn ripens fast in June. This is especially true when you water it well, which indeed you must at this critical period. If the kernels are plump and hard and your thumbnail doesn't make much impression on them, you've lost the best. Don't give up, though. Today's varieties are super-sweet and you can enjoy them after the usual prime condition. In fact, some varieties don't need any cooking. Shave off the kernels and eat them raw in a salad or, if you are under age, take the cob in both hands and bite away at the raw kernels. Don't waste water on a harvested corn plant—pull it out.

Plant sweet potatoes now. They love heat and sunshine. Not all nurseries stock young plants, so you may have to order from a catalog. Save some plants at harvest time and grow them during the winter as a houseplant in a sunny window. To learn how to do this, see page 143.

July

*J*uly is a month of false alarms. Thunder and lightning are common, but the promised rains don't always come as expected. Plants and people are under stress. Even desert plants show it; prickly pear pads shrivel and palo verde trees drop their leaves—until the rains arrive.

It's easy to jump to a wrong conclusion when something goes wrong with your plants this time of year. The symptom that first catches your eye—the sudden wilting of leaves that don't drop—could be caused by an excess of fertilizer, by herbicide chemicals, by grubs chewing on the roots, by overwatering, by poor drainage, by borers in the branches, by extensive cicada damage, or by sheer exhaustion. Or the soil could be dry. That's the possibility you should check first. It's the easiest to diagnose and you can quickly do something about it. Get out your trusty soil probe.

July can be a desperate time before the rains arrive. Temperatures reach 105F or more. Forceful winds break off tree limbs and hurl corn plants to the ground. Desert plants and animals suffer from dehydration and we humans tend to neglect things. It often rains on the Fourth of July—just to spoil those carefully arranged fireworks displays. But sometimes we're compensated with a free display of lightning and thunder that is just outside the window.

Palm tree flowers will soon turn into seeds and become a nuisance in the fall. Remove the flower stalks before they ripen.

🌱 Featured Plants for July

Saguaros

These noble desert natives can take the heat and arid conditions. If they shrivel and contract, don't worry. They'll fatten up as soon as the rains moisten the soil again. It is better to not water them or apply any fertilizer. In fact, saguaros should never be fertilized.

Be careful not to disturb the soil as far away from the plant as the plant is tall–even more distance is better. Saguaros have shallow roots that can be damaged by cars driving over the soil near them, or by bricking or cementing or from chemicals applied near them. Avoid the temptation to plant flowering plants around the base of plants. The amount of water that the flowers need to thrive could be deadly to the saguaro.

Birds peck away on the trunks and build their nests inside. This does far less damage than well-meaning gardeners inflict when they fill these holes with sand or try to cement them closed. However, wounds can go bad and if bacteria become established, the soft tissue can rot. Inspect saguaros in July. If you see a black fluid oozing from a new wound, scoop out the rotted flesh and leave the wound open to air to dry and heal. Spraying a solution of one part bleach to nine parts water will sanitize your work. The dry, black corky bark at the base of an old saguaro is nothing to worry about. (Also see page 47.)

Birds build nests in the "armpits" of saguaros–the area where the arm grows off the main trunk. In a wet year the materials in these nests can act as sponges, which enable molds to develop. For the sake of the saguaro, clear out these nests, even if there are birds in residence.

Palm Trees

Summer is a good time to plant palm trees or move them to another place but it's not a good time to prune them. Large palms are heavy plants and you may need a crane to lift them. (The trunks are full of water.) Although you'll remove most of the roots when transplanting, new ones will develop if the soil is warm. Maintain soil moisture. Protect the top of the palm with a cloth, or fold and tie up the fronds to shield the top from the sun.

Palm trees have a single bud. During a wet July, storms blow about fungus spores that can infect and kill the bud, thus the whole plant. This is perhaps the only reason to climb a palm tree this time of year— to apply a fungicide as a preventative. While you are up there cut out the long flower stalks that are now producing seeds. Palm seedlings are hard to remove once they germinate. Don't prune leaves and the protective leaf bases that cluster around the trunk. You'll expose the tree to July's intense sunshine, which can sunburn the trunk.

Soil Preparation

If you are following the soil sterilization program that you began in June, now is the time to remove the clear plastic. Dig the soil and cover again with the plastic, and leave in place through this month.

Planting

Final Vegetable Sowing

There's still time to get harvests from a last sowing of squash, corn and black-eyed peas in late July. It's risky to plant longer-term plants such as watermelons or cantaloupe. Corn grows well in the hot days of July and August, but we have to wait for cooler nights to be sure the pollen (necessary for kernel production) isn't killed. These will come in September and October.

Sow corn seeds now and sow again in three weeks, and even a third time another three weeks later. You'll get a good crop over a period of time that will include Thanksgiving and, with some luck, Christmas. Sow the seed in square plots rather than in long narrow rows. This increases the opportunity the pollen from the tassels will fall on a nearby silk and not be blown away by the wind.

Tomatoes

Your tomato plants are probably suffering in the July heat. Now is the time to cut back plants (about half of the top growth) so they will produce new fresh stems and leaves. Cover them with an old white sheet to keep the July sun from burning the newly exposed stems. This doesn't apply as much to the cherry types, but most other varieties look miserable in July and August. They just don't flower in the heat.

The new growth that follows will produce flowers that set fruit when the weather cools in September. Fruit production will continue until the first killing frost, most likely in November.

For a brand-new crop of tomato plants, sow tomato seeds in mid-July. They will germinate quickly and you will have plants big enough to set out in the garden in five weeks. Use a diluted solution of house-plant fertilizer in the water to complement the warmth that induces young plants to grow vigorously.

Because the days are warm in August and nights are beginning to cool, July-planted tomatoes grow exceptionally well. They start flowering in the cooler weather of September and produce good yields until frost rips them in November and December. Even then, it's possible to carry over young plants during a mild winter or protect them in a greenhouselike structure during a harder winter.

Order Cool-Season Vegetable Seeds

If you want to grow your own broccoli, cabbage, cauliflower, chard and other cool-season vegetables, a much wider range of varieties are available from catalogs as compared to the seed racks in stores. Place the order early this month and be prepared to sow seed early in August. Seedlings will be ready to set out in the garden the first half of October. Now is also the time to see that your coldframe or greenhouse is in good working order. See page 140.

♦ Watering

Continue to irrigate plants this month in spite of approaching rain. As you spend time in the desert, you quickly learn that summer rains are fickle and unreliable. Clouds build up beautifully, humidity increases, distant darkness and lightning are headed your way while great winds stir up dust, and the thunder seems loud enough to break the windows. Even with all this commotion you may not get a drop of rain. Then, finally, your patience is rewarded and the skies empty what seems to be buckets of rain. When this occurs you still have to remain skeptical. How much rain fell and how far into the soil did the moisture go?

This is a month when your soil probe becomes most useful. (See page 69.) Poke it into the soil to answer the water question. You are

Below: Small containers need daily watering during the summer months. Hook them up with a drip system working from a timer, but don't trip your guests!

Below right: If you water your container plants by hand, it might be time to abandon them for the summer.

likely to be disappointed. Summer storms are often all flash and crash with no substance. Keep on irrigating.

Irrigate Early

Irrigate plants early in the morning. You are preparing them for the hard day ahead, especially in the middle of the afternoon. An evening irrigation—after the plants have had a hard day—merely brings them back to their early morning condition. With trees and shrubs a substantial deep watering can be supplied any time of the day because it's designed to last more than a week.

Deep Watering

Advice is constantly given—perhaps to the point of irritation—to water trees and shrubs deeply. This is important, but people forget or they have misconceptions about the operation.

You frequently hear them say, "Of course I water deeply. I have a root feeder that goes down 3 feet. That's how far down you recommend, isn't it? I made it myself out of a piece of piping." Well, this is not deep watering, or at least not the best way. When you use one of these gadgets, you force water deep in the ground where it displaces soil and leaves great cavities. It should be called a *root disturber*. More often than not, it is the upper roots that don't get the water they need. In addition, a good watering moves salts down through the soil and away from the roots. You have to start at the top of the soil to achieve this. Deep-root feeders, or whatever they are called, have no place in desert gardening.

Beware of overwatering in the heat. You can feel the warmth in leaves when a plant is short of water. After an irrigation, the leaves transpire and the plant cools down, just as we perspire and cool down after a long drink. But we don't continue to cool down the more we drink; it's the same with plants. What's more, roots drown if they are kept too wet. The first sign of drowning is that leaves turn dull and droop. This is so similar to the symptom of plant stress caused by too little water that many people, particularly in July, rush to the garden hose. This leads to the second stage of stress caused by wet soil: leaves become chlorotic. Lawn grasses, for example, turn yellow. The cure is simple: Cut back on the watering. Use your soil probe regularly to determine if water is needed.

It's amazing how a tired lawn perks up after a good rainfall. When the summer rains finally start, turn off the sprinkler time clock to save water and to avoid fungus diseases. Get out the mower and make sure the blades are sharp. Mow the grass more often—about every four or five days. If you let grass grow tall and thick during the rains, it remains wet and fungus diseases can thrive.

A natural rainfall is worth ten irrigations. That may be a bit of an exaggeration, but a good rain does release a lot of growth energy. Don't push your luck by fertilizing a fast-growing lawn that already is dark green; its color tells you that it doesn't need nitrogen. If you give it more than it needs, it grows faster but weaker. It will exhaust itself and succumb to fungus attack.

Irrigate your lawn, when necessary, early in the morning. Sprinkling at night when humidity is high keeps the leaf blades wet and allows fungus diseases to spread rapidly.

Move plants in containers into a shady place. Don't put them completely under a tree because they need morning sunshine and afternoon shade. You may have to begin watering them every day.

Using Grey Water

Grey water is water that comes as a by-product of other use such as clothes washers and showers. Water from the shower won't hurt plants nor will water from clothes washing, provided it's free of sodium residues that are in some detergents. There's a conflict between water conservationists and health departments, who declare the dangers of using grey water. In fact, many cities forbid the use of such water. But people do. And the laws may be amended as our region becomes drier and drier.

If you do use grey water, avoid applying it in the same location on a regular basis. As a rule, use it up to one for every three irrigations so calcium residues won't build up. The same is true for recycling swimming pool water. See page 95 for more information.

Fertilizing

Fertilizing during the summer does have a place in our desert world. We water a lot, and as we wash down the harmful salts, we are also

If you decide to trim a hedge, make the base a bit wider than the top so that sunlight can reach all the branches. An overhanging top shades the lower branches, causing them to die, leaving gaps in the hedge. Tie a string to two stakes to use as a base line. Set the frame against it and trim all shoots outside of the slanting upright.

washing down the fertilizers we put there earlier to benefit plants. If we don't replace them now when growing plants need them most, we get pale lawns, sickly looking foliage and trees that lose their vigor and strength.

Before fertilizing plants, moisten the soil with about half the irrigation amount. Apply fertilizer and continue with the second half of the irrigation. If you throw dry fertilizer onto dry soil and hope the rain will wash it down, you may be in for a nasty surprise. Rain may not materialize and the fertilizer will be wasted. Or rainfall will be slight, causing the fertilizer to be carried to the roots in concentrated amounts that can injure them. Or a lot of rain might fall and the fertilizer will be washed away in the surface runoff. Although it's welcome, seldom does rain fall in the way we want it to during summer months.

Pruning

Leave the pruning shears and loppers in the shed this month. The exception is when plants are damaged by high winds; split, broken branches should be removed as soon as possible. Also remove wayward branches on shaped hedges. Trim lightly because heavy pruning can expose once shaded bark to intense sunlight, causing sunburn.

Pests and Problems

Grape-Leaf Skeletonizer

Be on constant alert for grape-leaf skeletonizer moths. See page 59. They come and go and even seem to disappear for a while, but they will be back.

Leafhoppers on Grapes

The tiny leafhopper is also a summer-long problem on grapes. There are always lots of them. Their rasping on leaves to get moisture and food causes the leaves to brown out. If infestations are heavy, leaves drop from the plant. Weekly sprays of diazinon will protect your grapevines from both pests. If you paper-bagged the bunches, you can safely eat the fruit soon after spraying and whenever grapes are ripe. Follow label directions to be sure it is safe.

Palo Verde Borer Beetle

We seldom see the Mexican palo verde borer beetle grub. It is bigger than your little finger and efficient at destroying roots. It lives in the ground for a year or two, eating the roots of many soft-wooded trees and shrubs, although the palo verde tree is the most common victim. Other favorites include mulberry, oleander, peach and plum. Trees that have been pushed along in their growth by frequent watering and heavy fertilizing so their wood is soft are more likely to suffer than trees living a more spartan existence.

The first noticeable sign of borer damage is dieback of branches and limbs, which turn light and then dark brown. After the soil has been thoroughly soaked and a gusty storm has blown an infested tree over, you see the chewed-over roots. At this point, it's much too late to save the tree.

When the thunderstorms of July beat their tattoo on the ground, the 3-inch adult brown beetle with prominent feelers emerges, leaving a hole the diameter of a broomstick handle. During its evening flight, it clumsily bangs against porch lights, crashes into the reflected light from swimming pools, and bumps into newly arrived desert dwellers sitting on the patio. They fly around for a week or two, find a mate, lay eggs and return to the soil—sometimes down the very same hole they came out of. Then they die. Their eggs hatch and turn into grubs that burrow down in the moist soil until they find a root where they start feeding. One grub won't harm the tree very much but palo verde borer beetles don't travel alone.

Where do they come from? Some years they are very common and are in everyone's yard. Other years it is hard to find one. All through the year they live underground as fat white grubs—the largest grubs this side of the Pecos.

A tree that is short of roots—for any reason—becomes a dry tree and loses its leaves. Twig ends die back, then the branches, then the limbs. In a year, the tree is dead, but you can't see the borers and you may not suspect their presence on the roots. The symptoms are common to many problems.

It's almost impossible to dig down into the soil after grubs, large as they are, to find the evidence. You destroy the tree in the process. Wait for the summer rains to see whether great holes appear under the canopy of your tree. Holes the size of a little finger appear at this time, too. Cicada grubs, turning into adults and crawling out in just the same way, cause them.

The treatment to combat palo verde borer beetles is a hit-and-miss operation, rather like throwing depth charges into the ocean to destroy a submarine you think is there. First, set a sprinkler halfway between the trunk and the ends of the branches. Let it run long enough so you can easily poke a probe 18 inches into the soil. Move the sprinkler to the other side of the tree and repeat the process.

Next, sprinkle diazinon granules over the wet ground. Follow the directions on the product label to know how much to use. Scatter ammonium sulphate over the same area at the rate of 1 pound to every 100 square feet. Water again to wash these chemicals deep into the soil. When you can poke your soil probe 3 feet into the ground, you've sprinkled enough. In any event, the watering you give the tree will help it, as will the ammonium sulphate, which encourages root renewal.

It may satisfy you to pour liquid diazinon, diluted according to the label directions, down the holes. Don't forget that these are exit holes, showing where the beetle emerged. It's only by chance the beetles are down there. But if one is down there laying eggs, the diazinon will take care of the next generation.

Leafcutter Bees

When you spot leaves of your plants that have neat circles and semicircles cut out of them, it's a sure sign you're garden has been visited by leafcutter bees. They prefer tender leaves, working very quickly to remove a circular portion. They use the leaves to build their nest, which is usually located in a small, narrow opening. Don't be too concerned. Although their "pruning" affects a plant's appearance, plant health it not usually threatened.

Green Fruit Beetles

It's the season for the green fruit beetle, that iridescent beauty that destroys ripening fruit. The best way to avoid this pest is to plant varieties of fruit trees that ripen before the beetles appear in July. However, your trees may have been planted by someone else and now you must live with the consequences.

Cover your trees with a sheet and spray the searching beetles with diazinon or Malathion 50® as they fly onto the sheet. Remove and discard damaged fruit as soon as you see them; they send out attractive smells to insect pests. Green fruit beetles are slow flyers, making a great whirring sound as they go. You can swat them with an old tennis racquet if you want some exercise. One inventive gardener sucks them off his fruit with a vacuum cleaner. (But you must empty the beetles out of the paper vacuum bag or they'll quickly chew their way out!) Dump them into a bucket of water and give them a drowning lesson. That way, you know where they've gone.

These beetles spend most of their lives as 2-inch-long, white grubs, eating decaying organic material. They are in almost every compost pile. When you discover them and place them on the ground in what you think is the right way—legs down—they roll over and wriggle along on their backs.

After that little trick, they stop being interesting. Put them back in the compost pile where they can chew up the bigger bits, but don't let them reach maturity and become a nuisance as a flying adult. Maybe it's best to feed them to the chickens. They're a delicacy, judging by the way chickens go for them. Or you can simply squash them.

Leaf-Footed Plant Bug

Another insect pest active in July is the leaf-footed plant bug. The first part of its name is easy to understand when you look at the flattened

For most of its life the large brown beetle called palo verde borer beetle lives as a grub feeding on the roots of plants. Any soft-wooded plant will do and the Mexican palo verde is perhaps the softest. One or two grubs won't hurt but if trees lose a lot of roots they will die, or get blown over in summer storms. The grubs turn into adults during the summer rains and climb out of the ground, leaving a large hole. Usually there's nothing in the holes by the time you see them.

hind legs. Being a bug, it sucks plant juices and, if this weren't enough, it introduces bacteria into fruit as it pierces the skin. This accounts for rotted fruit and spotty pecan nuts later.

When this pest clusters on pomegranates, tomatoes, late peaches or grapes, use the same protection methods as you do for green fruit beetles. Above all, don't let rotten fruit put out a smell.

Declining Cucumbers

Due to the hot weather, cucumbers begin to decline, even those in the shade. The summer sun is too fierce. If your plants are producing some fruit, they are likely to be bitter. No one is quite sure why, and there's no antidote. Some kinds are worse than others. The best variety for the desert is Armenian. It's a big fruit—although it's better not to let them grow big—and sometimes the skin is thick. All other kinds are a summer disappointment.

Texas Root Rot

Just to round out the bad news, this is the time of year Texas root rot is most likely to make an appearance. Texas root rot is a fungus in the soil and perhaps on the tree's roots all the time. A vigorous tree tolerates it until conditions become too stressful, then the fungus is able to overcome its host. It usually appears during periods of high temperatures and heavy rains that keep the soil wet too long—July and August.

To help avoid conditions that promote this disease, don't water trees on the same schedule as May and June. If the rains are heavy and continuous, turn off the automatic controls and water by hand according to the condition of the soil. Use the soil probe to guide you. If your trees show symptoms, carry out the following treatment at once. Delaying treatment can be fatal to your tree.

If you're certain your soil has Texas root rot after a root examination and a clinical test, you can choose to treat the soil to save the afflicted plant or plants. The treatment is simple; your goal is to make the soil more acid. This in turn suppresses the Texas root rot fungus, which prefers an alkaline soil, and makes the soil more favorable for another soil fungus that parasitizes the pest. The ammonium sulphate also provides nutrients to the tree, which gives it a chance to "grow out" of the problem. Treat when you anticipate an attack as well as when a plant suddenly shows the symptoms.

First, spread 2 inches of steer manure or compost (not peat moss or "mulch") on the ground beneath the tree in an area that extends a bit beyond the spread of the branches. Scatter 1 pound of ammonium sulphate and 1 pound of soil sulphur for every 10 square feet of manure. Dig these into the soil, being careful to avoid chopping the plant's roots. Water heavily. Use your soil probe to be sure you've watered these amendments in to a depth of 3 feet. Although there's the risk of keeping the soil too wet, which favors the fungus, irrigate deeply every two weeks unless it is raining heavily.

Measure all amounts—don't guess. The amounts of amendments necessary to kill the fungus are almost enough to kill the tree. Calculate how many square feet of ground you are going to treat and

The circular cuts removed from this rose plant show that the leaf-cutter bee has been at work. She flies in quickly and removes pieces of leaves, which she uses to line her nest.

weigh out the ammonium sulphate and sulphur. If you apply too little, the treatment will not be effective. If you apply too much, you might harm those roots that were not killed by the fungus. If you overdose on amendments and don't apply enough water, you can cause damage.

Plants afflicted with Texas root rot lose a fair portion of their roots. Dead, brown leaves appeared because the tree was unable to get moisture from the soil to its leaves and branches. The branches aren't dead and they will try to put out new leaves, but this effort will exhaust the tree. Save its energy and help it recover by removing all marginally useful branches. Your tree will look like a blasted skeleton, but you may have saved it. If so, it will recover its vigor in due course.

Weed Control With Preemergents

If you use them, apply preemergence weed killers before summer rains. The success of this treatment lies in getting the chemical in contact with the dormant seeds before they swell with moisture and begins to germinate. *Preemergence* is what it's called, but it would be a better reminder to landscapers and homeowners if it were called *prerain*. If you apply it a week before the rains come, it will wait in the soil for the seeds to begin germinating. In fact, preemergents remain viable for four or five weeks after they are applied. But be forewarned: if you apply it even one week after the seedlings begin to show, it won't work.

Fruit Split

During last month's dryness and increasing heat, fruit trees were under stress. In spite of irrigations, fruits hardened in the strong sunshine; they became corky and inelastic. Now comes the rain; all of a sudden trees gather up an enormous amount of moisture. A lot of this goes to the young oranges, pomegranates and peaches. The hard skin can't expand, the inside swells fast, and something has to give. The fruit splits. There's not much you can do to prevent this, even with liberal prerain irrigations. And there's nothing you can do after it's happened, except to remove the damaged fruit. If you leave them, they will attract flies and leaf-footed plant bugs.

Protect Fruit from Birds

If you want to enjoy your fruit crops, you must keep the birds away. You see them around during the heat of the day. They are invariably after your grapes, tomatoes, apples, peaches or figs—anything that's moist and juicy. This means putting paper bags on bunches of grapes and covering your fruit trees with a white sheet. This keeps the sun off the fruit as well as hiding it from the birds.

✓ Special Considerations

Harvesting the Rain

Water bills can run high the next three months. Plants must receive irrigation but homeowners look for ways to keep those bills reasonable. When the summer rains come, they come with a bang and much of the water runs off, instead of soaking into the soil as do the winter rains. If you have sloping ground on your landscape, you can take advantage of this free water. Channel rainfall from downspouts to groups of trees and shrubs. Or locate plants where you know water can be directed. Runoff from driveways, patios, walkways and the like can be channeled to plants.

Water harvesting from the roof is a good idea but its success depends on having a substantial storage basin. Some homeowners have even invested in large underground storage tanks with submersible pumps.

Storm Damage

Wind damage is a common problem in July. If your trees become heavy with rain and the winds are flying, it's likely that branches will be broken. If young trees are not staked, they may be blown over. A corn patch can be lying on the ground after a storm. Tall palm trees are often struck by lightning, which kills the tree, and there's nothing to do except have it cut down and hauled away.

Remove damaged limbs and branches of trees and treat cuts with pruning paint. It's seldom worthwhile to try to repair a broken branch. Even if it mends after being bound up, a weak spot remains in the tree branch. The branch split because it was weak in the first place so it's best to prune it out. Make a clean cut so that no stub is left, then apply pruning paint. If your tree is laden with fruit that you want to harvest, prop up the heavily laden branches with a couple of forked poles until the crop ripens.

Summer rains that keep the soil moist and soft, coupled with strong winds, quickly expose inadequacies of planting. The soil preparation here was skimpy and the planting hole was small. And because the irrigation system delivered water too close to the trunk, there was no spread of roots. The matter is further complicated by luxuriant top growth aided, perhaps, by liberal fertilizing and a lack of selective pruning.

A Case for Summer Pruning

Our January pruning caused additional growth, and that's the way we wanted it. However, much of that growth was renewal of leaf branches that will produce fruit next year. If too much grew, aided perhaps by liberal fertilizing and watering, the thick foliage won't let the wind blow through the tree. It gathers the force of the wind like a sail on a boat. Trees with underdeveloped root systems are often blown over. Before summer storms get started, carefully thin out any congested new growth on trees.

If a July storm pushes a small tree over, there's a good chance you can right it. To bring it back upright, first soak the soil to the point of making it a mud pie. Loosely but firmly pack the trunk with soft cloths against a 2 by 6 piece of lumber at several places. Then gently and gradually pull the tree upright again. (This may take two or three days.) If you can't do this manually, rent or borrow a ratchet "come-along" device. Attach it to the 2 by 6 so that you don't damage the tree's trunk. The anchoring end, of course, should be attached to something very stable. For example, you don't want your tree to topple a patio support pillar as you tighten the cable!

Rainfall and Mushrooms

If rain does fall, it's common to see a lot of new mushrooms on the lawn. Usually they are edible meadow mushrooms, but be quite certain they are not poisonous toadstools before you prepare your free meal.

In desert regions, tomato plants are allowed to grow unchecked, which is quite different from the pruned and caged plants in the East. The majority of tomato fruits are borne inside the foliage, where they are protected from the sun's scalding rays. The additional humidity also keeps the skin of the fruits soft.

July
In Your Garden

Mushrooms and toadstools don't parasitize your plants; they grow on the organic matter in the soil. Unless you are afraid of them or have small children, there's no need to get rid of them.

Creating Shade to Avoid Sunburn

July is supposed to be a rainy month, but in between the storms you can depend on strong, damaging sunshine. It's one of the reasons we shouldn't plant against the western walls of houses. Sunburn on leaves of evergreen plants such as citrus, privet and euonymus is common in July. Likewise, ripening fruit can be sunburned and spoiled unless we shade it. A bronze center on a leaf is the sign to fear. Trees that are short of water, even for an hour or two, sunburn most readily. Don't wait for them to wilt. You can easily feel the heat on their surfaces and that's the signal to give them a good watering. Trees are like humans; they cool by sweating, so they must have the moisture to enable them to sweat comfortably. Lay muslin, sheets, cheesecloth or old lacy curtains directly on the plants if you don't have the time and energy to make a supporting sunscreen frame.

Sunburn on grapes can be prevented by putting them in paper bags. You've probably already done this to thwart the birds. Apples, peaches and figs are not as easy to protect. Drape with cheesecloth coverings and be diligent about putting it back when winds blow it off.

Sunburn on fruit and vegetables can sometimes be prevented by selecting adapted varieties. A particular quality is the plant's ability to shade its fruit with its own foliage. As you study the seed catalogs before deciding which varieties to order, pay attention to this characteristic. Color photographs of plants grown in cooler climates may show plants with brightly colored fruit, sticking up in the air for all to see. During a desert July and August, you'll soon wish you hadn't bought such varieties, and realize the importance of this self-shading factor. Also avoid growing late-maturing varieties, which must live through the long, hot summer before we can harvest them.

Harvesting Fruit

Beauty Seedless and Perlette grapes are the first of the fruit harvest to be ready. Enjoy them. Anna and Ein Sheimer apples are also ready to pick during July. Don't leave them on the tree to get bigger, but eat Anna fruit while they have a pink *bloom.* Harvest before they turn a dull yellow. They are not good keepers even in the best of years. Ein Sheimer are smaller, greener and have a tart flavor that is better for cooking. Hot sunshine on ripe fruit accelerates its maturity to the point that it can spoil on the tree. While on this subject, be sure to collect and dispose of fallen fruit as you see it. It puts out a strong smell that attracts birds and insects.

On the joyous side of July, many beginning gardeners want to know when their vining fruits are ready to harvest. Often they pick a cantaloupe before it is ripe in a frenzy of self-satisfaction that quickly turns to disappointment. It's wise to follow this general rule: don't be in a hurry to harvest. The longer fruit remains on the plant, the sweeter it will be. There are always exceptions. Get eggplant before they lose their shine, regardless of their size. Harvest summer squash a day or two after the flower fades, when they are 4 to 6 inches long.

Cantaloupe are the easiest to judge ripeness. The veins on the skin become more prominent as the fruit turns from green to golden. When it is ready for harvest, it detaches itself from the stalk when you gently roll it along the ground. It *slips*—as the professionals say. If you have to tug to get it free, you will have an unripe cantaloupe on your hands.

Watermelon are the next easiest, although it calls for some scientific observation. For a few days, you've probably been thinking it's time to get that monster. You've placed it on a board to keep it out of the mud and you are fattening it with generous irrigations. The underside is white and flat. You're ready to do it. Don't! Size alone is no indication of ripeness.

Watermelons have little tendrils all along their vines. Use these as ripeness indicators. Close to where the fruit is attached, you'll find a dried-up tendril. It looks somewhat like a brown little pig's tail. Look back on the vine, away from the fruit, and toward the root. You'll see more of these tendrils. If there are three that are hard, dry, brown and curled, you have a ripe watermelon.

Ripeness in casabas, crenshaws and honeydews is not easy to judge, but here are some ideas. Press the end of the fruit where the flower was—the end away from the vine attachment—and if it gives a little, the fruit is ripe. Smell the fruit early in the morning when it's cool. If it's more aromatic than fruit in the supermarket, pick it. If the bottom starts to flatten where it lays on the ground, it must be getting soft and is ready to harvest.

But don't be in a hurry—and don't worry if you make a mistake. Even the experts are confounded in their efforts to harvest melons at peak flavor.

Human Concerns

Take it easy in July; you're under stress too. Don't tackle any great garden enterprises this month. It's not the best time of the year for planting or digging. Consider July a time for regular maintenance and watching for trouble. Trouble can include insect activity, germinating weeds, chlorosis and fungus diseases. By being observant and taking care of trouble in its early stages, you can save yourself work and perhaps save the life of valuable plants. If you have to do anything strenuous, such as repairing storm damage, take care of it early in the morning. This is when temperatures are cooler and we have the most energy. It's also the time when plants have their best moments. Make a point of inspecting plants in the late afternoon when they are the most stressed. Their condition at that time of day, the worst time of all, will immediately tell you whether the soil has enough moisture.

July
In Your Garden

August

*O*nly one more month of intense heat to go! This thought occupies every gardener's mind in August. Nothing can be worse than this heat. Just thinking about the cooler September weather keeps us going.

August is a continuation of July, but the weather is more intense: it's hotter, it's more humid, the insects have multiplied, and the diseases have taken hold. Storms are violent and they continue to be unreliable in location and delivery. Everyone but you seems to get the much-needed rain. Because of the increased humidity, it's uncomfortable. If you can afford it, it's a good month to take your vacation.

Most gardens look a mess in August. If anything has gone wrong, it's now magnified. Plants wilt at noon— even those that are believed to like the heat. If you don't provide a timely irrigation, they won't come out of the wilt and you may lose them. Pay special attention to plants in containers. Some must be watered twice a day.

August can bring a dismal end to the summer garden. Squash plants devastated by the vine borer and tomato plants turned brown by the heat are common signs of plans gone wrong. But August is also the beginning of another growing season, so we can take heart. All of a sudden gardening tasks take over our lives. There's tidying up to be done, planting beds to be dug. Soil mixes are prepared and poured into styrofoam coffee cups to become short-term homes to seed-sown plants. Some seeds can go directly into the garden. If we can find bedding plants at the nurseries, we set them out, too.

Italian cypress trees may "come apart" in August storms. The remedy is to bind up the loose branches with light rope, starting at the base and spiraling upwards.

🌿 Featured Plants for August

Citrus—Look for New Growth

The rains encourage citrus to produce flowers. This is exciting, but they usually drop off and don't set fruit—especially young trees. Those that do set on the larger trees account for the out-of-season lemons and oranges we find six months later.

New leaf shoots accompany the flowers and they grow well if the rains continue and humidity stays high. It's important to keep these tender shoots growing. If rain showers are sporadic, you will need to irrigate. Don't let this fresh new growth wilt during dry periods between showers. There's a temptation to hope that enough rain fell last time and the next shower will come tomorrow, but this is seldom the case.

Squash and Cucumbers

The beginning of August gives you an opportunity to sow the last of a series of squash seed that gave you harvests all through summer. The end of the month is too late to plant for guaranteed results.

It's worth taking a chance with the squash relative, cucumber. Bear in mind that strong winds may be with us through the end of September. Cucumbers, with their great, paper-thin leaves, need a location sheltered from bright afternoon sun. You'll discover the phrase "cool as a cucumber" has meaning with the way the plant grows. Our summer heat is usually too much for it.

Sow seed directly into the ground at the end of the month and give the seedling shoots something to climb—they'll grow up to 6 feet high. Growth will slow with October's cooler nights. The first frost in November will kill the plants. However, there's enough time for good harvests. It's worth trying varieties other than Armenian. They won't be bitter tasting during early fall weather.

Chinese Pole Beans

Keep picking the Chinese pole beans, also called yard-long beans. They are at peak production in August. The more you pick, the more the plants will produce. It's as if you are having a contest in which the plants always win. You cannot suppress their enthusiasm, so pick two or three times a week. Don't leave old pods on the vine to dry out, split and scatter seed. This tends to slow flowering and production almost stops. Chinese pole beans will continue to produce abundantly until November's first killing frost. It's worth the gamble to sow a few seeds now to augment your existing crop.

Pecan Trees

Pecan trees show a bad side to their nature in August, but it's not their fault. The developing crop needs a lot of water for the small nuts to ripen and increase in size. The insecure nuts show their dissatisfaction with life by dropping off the tree. It may be that they weren't properly pollinated or perhaps they were damaged by insects. Perhaps the tree

Beautiful clouds like this herald the arrival of summer rains.

is short of zinc or there could be just too many of them for the tree to carry during this stressful month.

Nut fall can also happen if a well-loaded tree becomes short of water. Then it becomes your mistake for thinking that the last storm gave the soil a good soaking when it merely wet the top 3 inches. You might also have been counting on the next good shower that has yet to come.

Pick up some of these fallen nuts and cut them open. Most likely they will be shriveled and half-formed—a result of earlier water shortage or poor pollination. If the nuts are dark spotted, it is because the leaf-footed plant bug got to them when the nuts were soft. The bug's piercing mouth parts allowed bacteria to enter and cause a localized rot. If the nuts are dark and shriveled, the tree is probably zinc deficient. In which case make a note to apply a spray of zinc sulphate on the new, emerging leaves next spring.

Sometimes the ground appears to be completely covered with fallen nuts. Recover your composure by looking up into the tree, where you'll probably see lots of good nuts still attached. But nut fall is a warning. Irrigate your trees generously from now until the husks start to turn brown, which indicates the insides have developed well and the harvest is at hand. Water so that moisture reaches 3 feet deep. Apply at the tree's *dripline* (and beyond), the area at the ends of the branches.

Tomatoes: Cut Them Back

If you haven't already done it, cut back tomato plants by mid-month. If you delay any longer, there won't be enough time for plants to regrow new foliage, produce flowers in the cool of the year—yes, it is going to be cooler in September and October—and set ripe, red fruit before frost kills the plants.

Spread the long branches of cherry-fruited types on the ground, radiating outward from the center. Where the stems have lost their leaves, dig small trenches and lay the stems in them. Cover with soil but leave the green, leafy ends out in the sunshine. Water widely to encourage the stems to grow new roots. Apply Miracle-Gro® at alternate waterings.

Use the trimmings to make new plants. Take a strong axillary shoot—one that has developed against the stem where an old leaf stalk is located—and cut it cleanly. It will be about 6 inches long. Dip the end in RooTone® powder and set it in a large styrofoam coffee cup filled with a light, sterile soil mix. Place in a location where it will receive bright but not direct sunshine all day. It will grow roots in a couple of weeks. It will be ready to plant in the ground at the beginning of September, but be ready to protect plants from frost in early November.

Roses

Roses take a rest in August. There's not much to be done about it, either, except to be careful with your sympathy. Don't give them "food" and don't keep them too wet. Just be content to get them safely through the rest of summer. If you planted some on the west side of your house—the worst exposure for roses—cover them with a white sheet to throw off some of the sun's radiation.

Irises rest in August, too. Beautiful as iris flowers are, they often are damaged by a late spring frost or gusty winds. The leaves, however, last most of the year as a bright green accent in the landscape. In August, irises begin to brown out and wither. Accommodate this natural tendency by withholding water and allowing the tops to die down completely. Don't worry; they're not dead. They simply need a rest.

Bedding Plants

Flowerbeds take a beating in August. The heat and bright sunshine can be deadly to shallow-rooted bedding plants. It's the end of their season and it's not worth fussing with them. It's too late to fill in gaps where plants have died and the whole bed is due for replacement soon. The most you can do for these plants is to remove dead flower heads in the hope that new ones will replace them. But don't expect too much due to the August heat.

Geraniums

Many geraniums rot out in the summer because of overwatering, but if yours are still alive, go easy on them until the weather cools. There's a strong temptation to help them along with liberal waterings, but that is the worst thing you can do. Don't worry about leaves falling off. Bare stems will send out new leaves when the weather improves. Cut back stems halfway at the end of August. If you like, root cut pieces in pots of perlite and vermiculite to make new plants.

Lawns

Modify lawn-mowing schedules to match grass growth, just as you did last month. Reduce the interval to five days, or possibly four. Your goal is to remove a small amount of new growth, about one-quarter of the total height, with each mowing. Don't mow too close to the ground. Leave a couple of inches of grass blades to shield the soil and roots from strong sun.

Planting

Sow Cool-Season Vegetable Seeds

Sow cool-season vegetable seeds this month. Make a planting mix of equal parts sand, perlite, vermiculite and peat moss. Fill 4-inch pots with this mix and plant three seeds in a diagonal line in each container. Thin to one or two of the strongest plants when they begin to compete with one another. Grow in a greenhouse if you have one, coldframe or on a bench protected from harvester ants and birds. Place in a location where seedlings will receive full sun.

Watering

Rains may be plentiful in August, in which case you can turn off or reduce applications from your automatic irrigation system. Or showers may be so unreliable that you'll have to irrigate by hand between the time-clock applications. Only your soil probe can tell you. Remember, too, that heavy rains or repeated irrigations wash nitrogen out of the plant's root zone in the soil. You may need to replenish this nutrient in the form of ammonium sulphate.

Coping with the Heat

One of the best things you can do to lower plant temperatures is reducing how much sun shines on plant leaves. Covering tomatoes, peppers and eggplant with an old, white sheet is an effective and economical way to protect them from the sun.

There's a danger in thinking that supplying more water will bring down the plant's temperature. If you do keep watering every day, you may drown the roots. They must have oxygen to breathe. Without it, your plants will suffocate and die. Initial symptoms of root drowning are dull, dark-green leaves that soon become chlorotic. It's a common error to assume automatically that pale-green plants need iron.

An application of iron chelate may give a temporary improvement, but you can make a permanent change—as much as the weather will allow—by letting the soil dry out slightly. The next irrigation, water deeply but let the soil surface dry before the next session.

Reducing Surface Evaporation

Don't spray plant leaves in an attempt to cool it down. Water droplets act as magnifying lenses and cause blister spots. Also water high in salts leaves behind a corrosive residue on the foliage.

If rains are inadequate during a hot August, water conservation is a priority. How do we keep our water bills affordable? You can save water by reducing evaporation from the soil surface. Use your crop residues as mulches over the soil. For example, you may have lots of corn stalks that otherwise have no use make a superb mulch around plants. If you don't have such materials, buy a bale of straw and scatter it over the soil. And in the case of strawberries, lay materials over the plants as well to provide shade. It becomes effective when it's 3 or 4 inches thick. Don't pack it down; lightly toss it on plants and hope the summer storm winds won't blow it away. Put it back if they do.

Water Carefully to Avoid Split Fruit

August rains have another effect that has a nuisance value. Ripening

fruit splits. The hard outer skin of pomegranates doesn't stretch as the insides swell and the skin splits open. It also happens to citrus (especially navel oranges) and tomato fruit. Such fruit is ruined—it will not repair itself. Remove before it attracts a host of leaf-footed plant bugs.

Minimize this sort of waste by watering plants carefully during the early summer. If they become short of water, the hot sun and dry desert air makes the skin of fruit hard and rigid. Unfortunately, no matter how careful you are about watering, you must expect a certain amount of split fruit.

After you have harvested apples, peaches and grapes, you can stop being so attentive about irrigating, but you mustn't forget about it altogether. Trees and vines are no longer carrying a load of fruit that is 90 percent water, but they continue to grow so need regular water. Don't rely on it to be provided entirely by summer rains; they're too fickle.

Using Swimming-Pool Water for Irrigation

If you have a swimming pool, you may be able to use the backflush water on your plants. A swimming-pool supply store can test the water for total salts. If the figure is less than 800 parts per million, it should be safe to use on Bermudagrass lawns, eucalyptus trees and other arid-land plants.

If your swimming pool has not been emptied for several years, the water will be high in salts because of the evaporation that takes place every summer. If you use liquid chemicals to provide chlorine, it's likely that the salts contain sodium—something you don't want to put on any plants, any time. If you have been using solid chemicals, then the residues in the water are probably calcium salts, which are not nearly as bad a prospect. In any event, don't spill the backflush water on the same part of the garden every time. Move it around so you

Above left: Plants in containers are under extreme stress during the summer and require frequent watering. It's easy to overwater if drainage is restricted. Hot wet soil can be just as damaging to plants as hot dry soil.

Above: Moisture in the soil evaporates quickly in the summer months. A thick covering of straw, hay or compost helps retain moisture and keeps the sun's heat off the soil.

don't fill a parcel of soil with unwanted chemicals. And never apply pool water near acid-loving plants such as azaleas, gardenias and camellias.

Watering Container Plants

Hot dry air and winds wreak havoc on unprotected container plants. It's worthwhile taking a look around for a more sheltered place for them. Put them where they will be shaded in the afternoon. Check the soil's moisture at the beginning of the day and watch to see if plants wilt at midday.

Black plastic containers absorb heat from the sun to the extent that plant roots cook in hot, wet soil. You can get around this problem somewhat by painting the containers white or wrapping aluminum foil around them. But for best results, keep them out of the direct afternoon sun. If possible, move containers to an eastern exposure; avoid south and west exposures.

Fertilizing

August is an ideal time to test the latest fertilizer experiments from California. Grape researchers there assert that an application of nitrogen just after harvest ensures the nutrient reaches branches where it will be stored, ready for springtime growth. They argue that a conventional application in February hasn't time to reach the opening buds and feed the rapidly growing shoots. Consider trying this with your own plants and see if they do better. The next time you irrigate fruit trees and vines, pause at the halfway point and spread ammonium sulphate under the branches at the rate of one pound to every 100 square feet. Resume watering until you can push your soil probe 3 feet deep. August is the time to try this. Waiting until September or October is too near dormancy for deciduous plants.

✳ Pruning

Don't Top Trees or Trim Palms

During a lull in the storms, you may get a knock on the door from a young man who tries to talk you into having your trees *topped*. Don't let him. If, on the other hand, he wants to *thin* out the limbs, it might be worth listening to his pitch. Many trees blow over because their foliage canopy is too thick. It gathers the wind like a sail, especially if the foliage has thickened because of a previous topping. Thinning, not topping, is the proper preventative.

The same young man who knocked on your door asking to top your trees might come back and want to trim up your palm trees. Don't let him do that, either. The majority of these workers remove too many leaves. Any tree trimmer carrying fronds to the dump should be fined five dollars for each green leaf. Allow your tree to remain natural.

If it's a continuously wet summer, there's danger a fungus will be blown into the top of a palm, infecting the bud. A palm tree has only one bud. If it is destroyed, the palm is finished. The proper treatment in this case is to prevent infection by applying a copper Bordeaux solution to the top of your palm tree before the rains begin.

Palms reach high in the sky and can act as lightning conductors. A tree struck by lightning usually is killed. A tree expert, with his expensive equipment, will have to be called in to remove the palm little by little, starting at the top. Check your insurance policy to see whether your company will pay for the tree's removal. Use neighborhood safety as the reason for the request.

Trimming Hedges

All hedges, but especially oleanders and privets, exhibit a new burst of energy during summer rains. This growth will spoil the shape of a formal hedge. Give it a light trim every two weeks to even up the ragged top growth. Or save yourself a lot of work and allow the hedge to grow

Plants that love the heat, such as this rosemary, grow quickly this month. This is the time for a light pruning if you want a formal appearance and a thick profile. A straight cut across the top will do it.

Before grapes (or any fruit) ripen, hide them from birds. A large sheet over the whole plant will do but so will paper bags on individual clusters. Don't make "breathing" holes. They act as windows and let the birds see what's inside. If you wait to protect your fruit after the birds have discovered them they will tear open the paper bags. Don't use plastic bags because they cause the fruit to sweat and mold.

the way it wants to. You won't have to maintain it nearly as often unless it gets completely out of hand. If leaves are pale green, apply ammonium sulphate once a month.

Pests and Problems

Fruit Beetles

Figs, peaches, apples and grapes are ripening and humid breezes carry the smell of spoiled fruit downwind to the green fruit beetles. They come in droves, together with sour fruit beetles—those small, brown things that get into the open-ended figs and turn them sour.

Avoid these pests by being clean and tidy. Pick off and pick up all damaged fruit and discard them. You may not be able to smell such fruit, but the odor is a powerful attraction to insects who rely on smell for all of their activities.

Cover the tree or bag (paper not plastic) the fruit to keep the beetles out. Spray the insects with Malathion 50® or diazinon as they search for the hidden fruit. If they cluster anywhere, trap them before they get to your tree.

Insect traps are effective and easy to make. Take a 1-gallon jar or can and place a funnel-shaped piece of window screen at the opening. A pair of scissors cuts it easily. Fasten it with string or a rubber band. Put rotten fruit, watermelon rinds or fruit juice in the jar. Green fruit beetles will come with their friends, walk down the funnel to the opening, fall in and be unable to get out. Dispose of them and clean the jar. (Some gardeners think a smelly jar is more effective than a clean one.) Repeat until you have caught all the beetles in your neighborhood.

If all the gardeners in your area followed this plan of action for a few years, there would be far fewer green fruit beetles to worry about!

Cicadas

During one of your walks around your landscape, you might see a number of dead tips at the ends of branches. Brown dead leaves hang on the ends, attracting your attention. It's enough to give you a fright because during summer rains it's common to think these are signs of Texas root rot. These brown leaves look much like the beginning of that scourge. (See page 84.)

It's wise to be concerned because you need to be alert to the possibility. But when you take a closer look, you'll see the brown leaves are the result of some physical damage. The stalk on which the brown leaves hang has a neat series of 10 to 15 fine, sawtooth marks close together. Sometimes you may see little white grubs in the crevices.

These grubs are bad news, but you can breathe a sigh of relief at this relatively slight damage. It's not the deadly Texas root rot after all. The damage to the branches isn't that bad. The most negative aspect is that next year's generation of cicadas is on its way into the soil. The tree has been lightly pruned and it could even be considered beneficial because side shoots grow from such tip pruning.

Spray the ends of dead twigs with Malathion 50® or diazinon. Better still, cut the branches off, grubs and all. As with all insect pest management, take measures as soon as you accurately identify the source of the damage. The longer you wait, the more likely grubs have gone on their way to safety in the soil.

If July had its dry spells and the rains begin anew in August, expect a second crop of insect troubles. Newly moistened soil stimulates pupae of grape-leaf skeletonizers and squash-vine borers to wake up and emerge. The first signs of trouble are adults flying around looking for a place to lay their eggs. When you see them, start looking for their egg clusters. Rub them out between finger and thumb before they hatch and you won't have to apply chemicals.

Pine Decline

Apart from a general browning of the inside needles, which is normal and to be expected during the summer, Aleppo pines sometimes show hand-size patches of dead needles on the outer branches. The experts haven't found a specific reason for this condition, so it's called *summer stress* or *blight*. Let this telltale sign remind you to give your trees a good deep watering this month, even if it rains.

Another summer problem afflicting pines is eriophyid mites. You don't see them, but you see their damage. New growth at the ends of branches becomes deformed into a compact bunch of twisted needles. You see the same thing on Mexican palo verde trees. Control with a miticide spray. At the nursery, the product you want is sold as "mite killer" or similar name. Some contain nicotine so be careful when using it as a spray.

Mite-damaged foliage also can be clipped from trees. Put the pieces into a bag and close before disposing of it. Leaving infected branches on the ground will give the mites a chance to get back into the tree.

There is a branch nematode that infests pine trees, too. It's hard to say where it came from, but we know it is spread through urban areas by tree trimmers and their tools. The symptom is similar to that of summer blight, but nematode infestations don't clear up: It takes but a couple of months after infection for a perfectly healthy tree to turn

August
In Your Garden

completely brown and die. An infected tree should be removed and hauled away. In fact, the whole tree should be burned to kill the infestation, but local laws usually prevent this kind of cleanup. After cutting up the infected tree, disinfect your tools in a 10 percent bleach solution.

Harvester Ants

Harvester ants become busy in August. They strip leaves from plants and haul them back to their nest. They even appear to increase their numbers and start new nests. Their unrelenting industry—praised by Aesop—is a nuisance to desert gardeners and especially those gardeners who sow seeds in August.

These ants live in the ground but work on the leaves of your plants at night. Unless you are an early riser or inspect your plants at night by flashlight, you won't see them. However, harvester ants leave tell-tale trails of dropped bits of leaves to their nests. Blending a grapefruit into a mush and placing a handful at each hole has shown to be an effective organic treatment. The ants stop being a nuisance and perhaps go to the neighbors. Chemical treatments include pouring diluted diazinon or malathion down the hole, but a more effective treatment is Amdrol® pellets. Follow all directions on product labels. It may also be worth spraying the foliage of the plants they are attacking with Malathion® or diazinon before too much damage is done. Don't waste your time and energy filling the hole with water, or try to dig up the nest.

Weeds and More Weeds

Even fickle summer rains supply enough moisture to produce a great crop of weeds. The humidity stimulates them so much that they can easily grow head-high in undisturbed alleys and waste places. But not in your garden! Worry about these weeds because they are generating seeds for next year. Pull them up while the ground is soft. They come out easily, roots and all. If you put off the task and the soil dries, you're likely to snap them off at ground level. The roots will regenerate new shoots that produce seed close to the ground.

If the tall weeds that you pulled already have set seeds, it's foolish to leave them lying around to dry out. They will shed their seed where you let them lay. Don't be hasty in turning to chemical controls. Large weeds call for a lot of poison and there's the temptation to use something strong and final such as soil sterilants. They will do the job all right—and then some. Soil sterilants last up to 10 years and damage everything in their reach. This may mean your trees—and your neighbor's trees—as well as the soil itself. If you sterilize your garden soil, you automatically handicap yourself in any gardening activity for many years. The roots of your fruit trees may be in the alley with the roots of weeds. It's better to avoid using soil sterilants.

Small weeds quickly die if you hoe them in the midday heat. It's easy if the soil is moist at the surface and your hoe blade has a good cutting edge. Take a file and smooth edges until they are sharp enough to cut a piece of paper. Sharp tools make work a joy.

✓ Special Considerations

August is the prime time for desert gardeners to take a getaway vacation. Find somewhere cool and stay away as long as you can. But what will happen to your garden while you are away? Even with an automatic watering system there's a need for human surveillance. Something might break, storms may blow down trees, weeds may grow 6 feet tall with generous rains, and pests can consume half a garden while you are absent. In addition, a neglected landscape area advertises your absence just as much as a heap of newspapers or an overflowing mailbox. Find a caretaker to look after things while you are gone.

A Caretaker Checklist

If you have a friend who knows your gardening ways, there isn't a lot of preparation required. Perhaps all that's needed is a reminder list and a walk around the property before you go. On the other hand, if you are encouraging a young neighbor to enter the work force for the first time, it's only fair to train him or her for the responsibility.

You need someone who is reliable—not clever. It's a fact that young people are not experienced and that's nobody's fault. They are energetic and work on impulses. Consider making a list of things they *should not do* while you are away.

Likewise, make a list of what you want done and when. Take it with you as you do your walk, pointing out the jobs you want done. Actually show your helper how to do them. There may be some particular idiosyncrasy in your equipment, your way of doing things or the way a certain plant must be treated. Take this walk about a week before you leave. Your helper then has time to think about things and ask questions. Then, a day or so before you leave, go through the tasks again. Allow him to do the talking and you do the listening (don't interrupt) and you'll know if he has understood.

Stress the need for personal safety, especially if your caretaker will use power equipment. Here is a case where consultation with the parents is advisable. Do they approve of their child using unfamiliar power equipment, electric garden tools or chemicals?

Give full instructions on using your power equipment, and let him test it out. Don't let him use anything unless you are satisfied about his capabilities and the machine's performance.

There are two points of view about having friends over as he works. First, a friend may be able to help if something goes wrong. Second, friends are a distraction and temptation. Further, friends—especially young ones—are an added responsibility. They can easily be hurt if they get too close to things like a power lawn mower that throws out stones as fast as bullets.

It's a good practice to encourage conscientious work by giving a bonus if all is well on your return. Say this before you go, but be careful not to give the impression that you will give him more if he does more. He might do far more than you want.

August
In Your Garden

September

*I*n the landscaping year, September comes between harrowing summer and delightful fall. Unfortunately, September can't make up its mind. Fierce heat alternates with mild sunny days, but cool nights hint of things to come. The summer heat is gone—or going—yet there's warmth in the sunshine. What makes the difference between the summer misery and pleasant weeks of fall is the cooler nights. A difference of 20F between day and night temperatures allows us all to rest more comfortably at night and work better the next day. Recent research in plant science has shown that plants—even cotton plants that are considered to love the heat—do most of their body building during the night. This helps to explain why the fall weeks are productive.

   September can be rainy or dry, and it often is stormy. For landscapers and gardeners, it is a busy month full of opportunities. Just don't try to act on too many good ideas. It's your last chance to use the heat as an excuse to avoid hard work. There'll be plenty of time for that next month.

When preparing the soil for planting the fall garden, many gardeners prefer to use a garden fork for mixing and turning.

❧ Featured Plants for September

Sweet Corn

Don't underestimate the water needs of the corn you planted last month. Daytime temperatures reach 90F or sometimes much higher. Clear skies and the fact that evaporative coolers are working now to keep us comfortable tell us the air humidity is suddenly lower. Be alert and observant. Supply plants with good deep irrigations. You've got to keep your plants growing.

   When corn is knee-high, apply a side dressing of ammonium sulphate, about 1 pound to every 100 square feet. Water it in well. At this stage of growth expect damage from the stalk borer. The first sign of the grubs' activity is a series of holes in the new leaves as they unfold out of the funnel.

   Dust or spray a small amount of diazinon into the funnel of each plant before it reaches knee high. To be certain, give three applications, each a week apart.

   Corn cobs with open ends allow entry of corn earworm. Damage can be prevented by applying four or five drops of mineral oil when the silks are fresh and green. As soon as you see the silks coming out, make the application. Don't delay!

   Sow another plot of corn early this month to make sure of a Thanksgiving harvest. Plant your corn in square blocks rather than single rows. Pollen from the top tassels must fall onto the lower silks at the appropriate time—usually within a week—to develop a full cob of kernels. Wind blows pollen about so it is more likely to land on silks in a massed planting.

Sow Beans and Peas

Near the end of the month, sow large seeds of fava bean, horse bean or Italian bean, and those of English peas—including snap peas or Chinese edible-pod peas. They don't germinate well in hot soil so wait until your soil thermometer reads 70F when placed 2 inches deep. Bush beans that went in the ground earlier prefer a germination temperature of 80F. Any late sowing of these legumes will produce a slower germination as the days turn cooler. Complete your third sowing of bush beans in the series before the end of the month.

Keep picking your Chinese pole beans and you will be rewarded with an even greater production. The more you pick, the more you get. This is a truism for plants that produce fruit except, of course, the one-time blossoming and fruit set of trees.

Green or snap beans are best eaten before the soft pod develops any fruit. Yes, beans are a fruit—botanically speaking. Don't wait for the pods to get knobby enough to show the developing seeds inside unless you want a mess of soft-shell beans. Although beans germinate nicely, you may not get much of a harvest before the first killing frost strikes in November. Select short-term varieties such as Greencrop, Tender-Green, Greenpod and Tenderpod. Such similarity in their names suggests a commonality in their family history. They may not live up to their 55-day maturity as promised, but they'll come close to it.

Iris

September is iris-dividing time. Dig up big clumps and cut them into smaller pieces for replanting. Cut the fan-shaped leaves back to about 6 inches and clean away any dead leaves and rhizomes. If you're concerned about soil-borne diseases, wash the soil off the roots and dip them in a fungicidal solution before planting. While you're at it, examine the roots for maggots and throw the infested ones away. Plant the roots quite shallow, barely covering them with soil. Don't keep the soil too wet after planting. Irises grow out from the center of a clump so make sure the new pieces point outward. You want them to spread out and away from each other and not grow to create a tight mass. Avoid planting in the same location every year to reduce soil-borne diseases.

Prickly Pear

How do you tell when prickly pear fruit is ripe? It's the same story as with citrus fruit. Don't rely on last year's date but do a taste test. There's no magic date that tells you when to start making jellies—some years are early, others are later.

Winter Herbs

September is prime time to set out winter herbs. There are summer kinds and winter kinds, and we should switch out our herbs as the seasons change just as we do our flowers and vegetables.

A suitable herb garden can be planted in a half-barrel—you don't need a lot of plants or space. It's better to buy plants from a nursery because it's far too troublesome to grow herbs from seed, although it can be done. Herbs like a sandy, well-drained soil and the half-barrel should be placed where it gets plenty of winter sunshine. They also like a free-draining soil that is not too rich. After plants are started, hold back on fertilizer. Most failures with herbs are usually attributed to giving them too much attention.

Parsley is a good herb to include in your half-barrel garden. It's ornamental and you can pick off the lower leaves as they become ready for salads or the cooking pot. Two or three plants will keep you in fresh nutritious, flavorful leaves through the winter. Parsley goes to seed and stops growing when mild spring temperatures turn to summer heat. Cilantro, or coriander, is another easy-to-grow winter herb. Others to try are chives, sage, thyme and oregano.

If you grow mints—including the common spearmints and peppermints—consider keeping the plants in their containers and plant them container and all in a half-barrel (see above). This keeps the roots self-contained. Otherwise plants intermingle to form an underground jumble that is hard to untangle. Mints like shade and plenty of moisture. A little houseplant fertilizer in the water helps new plants establish and grow well, but don't overdo it. Otherwise you'll get rank plants with poor aroma.

Like the mints, watercress also enjoys shade and moisture. You can buy a bunch of watercress in almost any supermarket. Take three or four of the strongest springs and set them in a glass of water on the windowsill. Keep the water fresh and you will have roots in four or five days. Plant the rooted cuttings in a 5-gallon bucket of just about any type soil and keep them well watered. Pick the leaves regularly and you'll get more and more growth. Eventually the top of the bucket will overflow with greenery. Watercress is high in vitamin C—as high as any fruit. Old leaves produce a strong mustardy flavor so seek out young leaves to liven up your sandwiches.

Tomato and Pepper Plants

Tomato and pepper plants recovering from the summer heat will benefit from a side dressing of ammonium sulphate. The beautiful weather encourages their growth. Help them by making sure they don't run out of nutrients. Most gardeners spent a lot of the summer irrigating extensively, which washes the soil clean of nitrogen. Tomato roots spread out wide—as much as the foliage before you cut plants back. (See page 92.) Scatter ammonium sulphate fertilizer over the entire root area. Each plant should get about one-half cup every two weeks. Dry fertilizer should always go on damp soil and washed down into the soil with a slow irrigation.

Strawberries—Time of Renewal

If you lost most of your strawberry plants during the summer—a common occurrence—dig up those that remain and plant in 6-inch pots. Without breaking them apart, carefully dig up those plants that have strong runners and a bunch of leaflets on their ends. Plant them in separate containers close to one another. Let the mother plant continue to nourish these young ones. Their "umbilical cords" will take nutrients from the mother plant to these baby plants until they grow their own roots and become independent. A tablespoon of balanced houseplant food in a gallon of water provides nutrients to encourage growth.

If you don't have enough strawberry plants of your own, you can try to find plants in the nurseries. As a rule they don't have suitable plants this time of year. If plants are available they are usually expensive. If you get plants from a friend, swap meet or patio sale, be aware of the risk of introducing soil-borne diseases into your garden. Toward the end of the month, plant your new strawberry bed.

Loose-Leaf Lettuce

Many varieties of lettuce grow well in the desert—all the looseleaf types, that is. Head lettuce is not easy to grow and is seldom worth the challenge.

Even after caring for lettuce seedlings and getting them successfully transplanted, they are not safe from sparrows or other birds. If you don't like the idea of growing lettuce to feed birds, protect seedlings by covering them with a frame of small-mesh chicken wire.

At the end of September set out your first-sown seedlings in garden plots. Work quickly and carefully in moist soil because the air is dry. Small plants lying out in the sunshine are sure to suffer if their roots are exposed to the air too long. Even a minute during midday is too long. The cool early evening hours are the best planting times because plants largely recover from transplant shock during the night.

Fava Beans and Garden Peas

Fava beans and garden peas will grow through a mild winter safely. You may sow their seed at the end of September and in October. They begin to flower in the spring—early spring if they grew without interference from frost, later if they were nipped.

Fava beans grow on a thick stalk to about 4 feet high and tend to have a short harvest period and then die. But they are good! Garden peas tend to produce over a longer period of time. They need a support for their growth, which can reach 6 feet high. The more you pick, the more they produce. It's possible to gather a light crop as late as the end of May before the heat kills off the plants. Both plants should be harvested before their pods turn dry and hard. The seeds inside are most tasty when they are immature.

Citrus and Grapes

Don't be surprised to see fresh growth in grapevines and on citrus trees. You might get a strong flowering along with new leaf shoots. Sometimes these flowers set fruit.

Lawns

There's more warm weather ahead, so don't be too hasty to overseed Bermudagrass lawns with ryegrass. Wait for soil temperatures of 75F. Don't change horses yet.

Fertilize summer lawns now. Several weeks of growing weather lie ahead. Every two weeks, apply 1 pound of ammonium sulphate for every 100 square feet of lawn and water it in well. Your lawn will green up quickly.

During a wet summer, lawns that are short of nitrogen will produce mushrooms. There's nothing wrong with them except they are unsightly and leave a dark, permanent "fairy ring" on the green grass. This is because the fungus provides nitrogen and greens up the circle of activity. Even out the different colors by top dressing the area with ammonium sulphate at the rate of 1 pound for every 100 square feet.

If your lawn has turned a yellow-green, it might be due to a lack of iron brought on by overwatering. Check for moisture with your soil probe; if the soil's too wet, let it dry out a bit. The grass will turn green again, all by itself and at no cost to you. If this doesn't work, add iron in the form of ferrous ammonium sulphate. Keep the crystals off the sidewalk and away from the pool because they can leave permanent, rusty brown stains.

Warm weather, ample moisture and fertilizer all lead to vigorous growth. Don't let the lawn get away from you. Maintain it at 2 inches high. If it grows much taller the grass shades itself too much. You want a lawn to go into winter as strong as possible. Continue irrigating Bermudagrass until it goes dormant and turns brown naturally, usually by mid-November. Stop irrigating at this point, then begin again in March. However, if you want to keep the lawn green you can overseed with annual ryegrass.

Roses

As soon as roses recover from the summer heat and start putting out new shoots, it's time to prune for flower production. Buds develop about 50 days after cutting the old canes. It will be cool then, and the flowers will unfold more slowly and last longer than they do in the quickly warming spring. Because pruning stimulates growth, give each pruned plant a half-pound of ammonium sulphate and water it in well.

Poinsettias

If you want a striking red display of poinsettias during the holidays, place them where they'll receive 12 or more hours of darkness each night for the next three of four weeks. Outdoor plants near a porch light or a street lamp will not perform nearly as well as those that receive complete darkness. Use a large cardboard box or light-proof cloth covering (a white sheet won't do) to ensure complete darkness at night. Start this operation early in September. At the beginning of the month, give the plant a light haircut, snipping the ends of all the branches. This trimming will stimulate dozens of new shoots. It's on new end growth that the colorful *bracts* (a modified flower) develop.

Red Bird of Paradise

Mexican, or red bird of paradise flowers strongly in September. During the next few weeks the flowerheads will produce brown seed pods. Trim them off in their early stages if you don't like them, and you'll most likely get more flowering from new shoots. If you prefer to save the seeds, let the pods stay on the plant until they are hard and brown. Just before they split open, cut them with long stalks and hang them in a paper bag in a dry place. After a few days the pods twist open and forcibly throw the seeds out. You can actually hear them banging away against the bag after the pods explode.

For faster germination than that provided by Mother Nature, file a nick in the brown coat, just enough to let you see a lighter color. File the side of the seed—not its edge—so that you won't damage the embryo. Sow seed 1 inch deep in a styrofoam cup filled with a light, sandy soil mix. Keep in a warm place and water regularly. When the plant is about 4 inches tall, move it into 1-gallon container filled with the same soil mix. A little judicious fertilizing (diluted houseplant fertilizer works well) will help it along. Continue to grow in a warm, sunny location. By late spring it will be ready to plant outside.

Soil Preparation

Dig the ground and prepare it for planting your fall vegetables and flowers. Many gardeners advise against using the same plot ground for same plants year after year. This is good advice because it gives your soil a rest. Plant a different crop and you won't be as likely to keep feeding verticillium wilt or other soil pests that will attack your plants.

As you dig, watch for Bermudagrass. Pull it out, roots and all. Pick and dispose of any grubs you turn up in the soil. Leave the soil to mellow with its newly added steer manure or compost, ammonium phosphate and sulphur (see above) before you set out plants. Seed sowing comes even later.

Planting

Planting the Fall and Winter Garden

In spite of the heat and humidity, September is an exciting month in the desert because it's time to plant the fall or winter garden. There's a lot of hope and optimism in the air. Fall and winter gardens are usually more successful than those in spring and summer. And this is leading to a trend. If you want to be selective in your gardening activities, join an ever-growing crowd of efficient gardeners who take it easy between June and August. It's very sensible of them, but they are not excused from gardening altogether. Their fruit trees and vines must be kept growing with regular irrigations, but these "new-wave" gardeners don't go looking for work.

Fall Gardeners

They believe it's not worth the water, work in the heat, fight against

It's hot, and work can be miserable in September, but it's time to prepare the soil for a fall garden. If you wait for cool weather the winter vegetables won't have enough time to mature before frost comes in November.

pests—and any other excuse that comes to mind—to produce an unreliable summer crop of tomatoes. They save their energies and garden space for fall and winter.

In September they clean up the summer weeds in their fallow gardens, add organic matter, ammonium phosphate and sulphur to the soil and dig the ground. There's no heart-wrenching decision to be made about saving exhausted summer plants in hope they'll produce something before frost.

They go to the nursery, buy a few tomato plants and set them out. There isn't enough time for peppers and eggplant, but short-season tomatoes will produce before frost if all goes well.

They sow sweet-corn seeds and bush beans in the newly dug ground. Any winter vegetable plants they find at the nursery get planted too, except lettuce. Planting lettuce before cool October weather can cause plants to produce bitter leaves.

They make a soil mix and fill up numerous coffee cups. Then they sow two seeds in each cup—only two. Conditions for germination are so good there's no need for pessimism.

They choose seeds of leafy winter vegetables—lettuce, cabbage, cauliflower and broccoli, for example—that will produce plants to set out into the garden in six or seven weeks.

They don't overlook the Oriental vegetables. These are refined versions of the cabbage family that have interesting flavors, and are

108 ❖ *September*

Seeds sown in coffee cups in August should now be growing strongly. Help them along by adding house-plant fertilizer to the water every other irrigation. Start with one teaspoon to one gallon of water when the plants have four leaves. Increase to a tablespoon when plants have six or eight leaves.

enjoyed by gourmet cooks. They are also easy to grow.

Those winter vegetables that produce roots are sown directly in the ground early in October after the soil has cooled a little. Garden peas and fava beans are planted now.

The shortness of the seasons makes it important to choose fast-growing varieties. You'll be able to make another sowing at the end of September and spread the harvest into December and even January—in spite of cold weather. These vegetables were developed to grow in places far colder than our mild desert winters. They grow quickly.

In early September the soil is so warm that seeds germinate quickly and plants grow rapidly. The nights are beginning to cool, so the plants are not under stress as they continue the hard work of growing.

There's a temptation to sow seed directly in the ground instead of going through the coffee-cup process. This saves work and perhaps time, but you may regret it if you take the short cut. Germinating seeds and the resulting seedlings are tender and fresh, and become tasty targets for birds, caterpillars, cutworms and particularly harvester ants. Covering the seedbed with small-mesh chicken wire provides some protection. If this is not enough, muslin or cheesecloth can be placed over the wire. Insect pests can be kept away with chemical sprays but ants are too numerous and persistent so you'll have to treat their nests to be effective. See page 128.

Flowerbeds

Although it is too early to set out cool-season bedding plants, it's a good time to clean up and dig organic matter, ammonium sulphate and sulphur into flowerbeds, so they'll be ready for an October planting.

Coffee-Cup Seedlings

Seeds sowed in coffee cups in August should now be growing strongly. Help them along by adding houseplant fertilizer to the water every other irrigation. Start with one teaspoon to a gallon of water when the plants have four leaves. Increase to a tablespoon when six or eight leaves appear. Plants will be big enough to set out at the end of the month. This means you should not delay in getting the soil ready.

Planting Deciduous Trees

If you are optimistic and you've taken care of your vegetables chores and want to do more, dig some planting holes for trees and shrubs. Admittedly, it's hard work, even if you start early in the morning, but the cooling weather makes it less taxing. Digging holes now is good preparation for some enjoyable planting this month and in October.

Before your enthusiasm evaporates, a hole for planting a tree should measure 5 feet square and be 5 feet deep. (See page 2 on how to prepare a planting hole.) And you must dig through any caliche you find. When you think you've dug enough, half-fill the hole with water and see if it has drained out by the morning. If it hasn't, there's more digging to be done to be sure the planting hole is well draining.

What's interesting about planting trees (or most other landscape plants) in September is that the soil does not cool as quickly as the air. The soil will stay warm enough to encourage new root growth, providing it is kept moist. This makes it an ideal time to establish deciduous trees. This is not true for evergreen citrus trees; they can't take freezes. But deciduous fruit trees are going to lose their leaves anyway, and they need cool weather to produce fruit.

Sow Seed of Sweet Peas

It seems an unlikely time for sowing spring flowers, but sweet peas are slow growers. Sow them now. The Spencer varieties of seed seem to do best. Not many nurseries carry them so you may have to order seed from a catalog. Second best are the more readily available "heat-resistant" varieties at your local nursery.

Choose a sunny spot and dig a trench 2 feet deep. Put 8 inches of steer manure in the trench then lightly scatter ammonium phosphate on this. Now cover the fertilizer with 8 inches of bagged garden mulch. Finally, add 2 inches of sandy soil on top of the trench. Don't mix these layers, even though doing so breaks all the rules of soil preparation. Give the trench a good soaking. Sow seed 1 inch deep 2 to 3 inches apart in the sandy soil; it is there to ensure good drainage for the daily waterings required until the seedlings emerge.

You'll notice that you still have about 4 inches of space left in your trench. Gradually fill in with leftover soil around plant stems as the plants grow. Fresh roots will develop from the stems as they are cov-

ered, increasing strength of the plants. Pinch out top leaves when stems are 6 inches high to create growth of strong side shoots.

With all that fertility in the root zone there should be no need to add additional nutrients. You'll need to provide climbing support for the plants before too long; don't wait until they fall over as they grab one another with their tendrils. You can start with chicken wire, but it will not support mature plants when the wind blows. Construction mesh, stood on its edge, is a good support.

Sow Seed of Winter Vegetables

Winter vegetables give us an opportunity to do some intensive planting, which, in turn, gives us an early harvest. Some of the best winter crops include beets, carrots, radishes, turnips, lettuce, cabbage and broccoli.

The trick is to sow seed thickly and directly in the garden as soon as you notice the ants have gone underground. A good way to get a well-distributed plant population is to press a rake into the soil until the teeth make 1/2-inch-deep holes. Pull the rake straight up without disturbing the row of holes and set it in again. You are making a series of holes in a square pattern throughout your bed. (See photo above.)

Sow one seed in each hole. Any of the winter vegetables are suitable, whether they are leafy kinds or root producers. The emerging seedlings will be about 1-1/2 inches from one another and will not become crowded for perhaps three or four weeks.

As soon as they touch one another, gently pull out the alternate plants and wash them ready for eating. Those that remain will grow stronger because the competition has been removed—for awhile. Keep thinning and eating as the seedlings grow. This method provides a quick and productive harvest from a small piece of ground. In due course, you finish with a harvest of full-size root and leaf plants. The bonus is that you get to eat the "gourmet" thinnings along the way.

Above left: Sweet peas grow well in containers. Give them sturdy supports and go vertical to save garden space.

Above: After you've added soil amendments and leveled the vegetable bed, use a rake to prepare the seedbed. Each hole is the same distance from the last one and you can regulate the depth according to the size of the seed. One seed per hole, please!

Planting in Containers

An easy way to gain additional garden space is to grow plants in containers. Slowly recovering pepper plants in your summer garden can be pruned back, dug up and put into 5-gallon buckets. During the forthcoming winter you can protect them from cold weather and freezes by moving them to a sunny part of the garden. The black buckets absorb the heat of the sun and the soil retains it through the night. If you have space for half barrels, you can make a summer-salad arrangement, mixing tomatoes, peppers, onions and lettuce in the same container. Or plant a winter herb garden, as described on page 103.

◊ Watering

A good storm at the end of summer may deliver a lot of water, but that doesn't mean the roots of your plants will get it. Summer rains, rightly called *gully washers,* often run off on the surface instead of soaking in. Use your soil probe after a downpour to find out what's happening underground. Don't use the color of the sky as an indicator of whether to irrigate or not.

A truly wet summer can be a real threat to the safety of your trees, too. If so, turn off your automatic irrigation system and water by hand. It's more work, but it may be necessary to save your trees. Overwatering can lead to root rot and tree loss. Whether storm clouds bring moisture or not, they invariably bring strong winds. Tend to wind-damaged trees quickly.

Reduce Water to Slow Growth in Fruit Trees

As we approach the end of the gardening season we want to avoid encouraging growth of established deciduous trees and vines. They need several weeks of dormancy and usually don't get enough winter chilling (cold temperatures below 40F) to reliably produce a crop of fruit.

The onset of cold weather usually nudges plants into dormancy. A way to substitute for insufficient cold is to reduce their water supply. This simple technique slows growth of grapevines, apricot and peach trees, for example. Use the same tactic with citrus trees to slow their growth and harden plant tissues in anticipation of a November or December freeze.

Continue to give deep irrigations, down to 3 feet, but gradually lengthen the interval between waterings. Maybe every three weeks will be enough. Let the surface of the soil stay dry longer, but watch the young growth on the citrus and don't allow it to wilt for more than a day. Although citrus fruit is ripening and filling with water, there is little risk of losing it at this stage of development. In fact, the fruit, being full of water, acts as a reservoir of moisture and saves your tree from drying out too much. But don't let the dryness go too far.

With deciduous fruit trees and grapes, you have a good indicator of readiness for rest in the leaf color. Once the color starts to turn, cut back on the water. A good soak at the end of September might be enough for the remainder of the winter. Use the soil probe to know for certain how deeply water is going into the soil.

Fertilizing

September is a time to renew lost fertility. Your landscape shrubs, trees, and vines want to grow in the cooler temperatures, and there are several weeks of good growing weather ahead. All they need is ammonium sulphate; you scatter it on the surface at the rate of 1 pound for every 100 square feet. Precede and follow with a good watering.

But be careful about fertilizing frost-tender plants. Winter is coming, and it might come early. You don't want frost-tender plants to be actively growing when the first nip arrives in November. Citrus, bougainvillaea, hibiscus, palms and a few others will put on a growth spurt during the next few weeks, but don't encourage them too much. By the end of September, your plants should gradually make the transition to a resting condition. Ignore the temptation to encourage growth fueled by an Indian summer.

Pruning

Oleander, privet, xylosma, Texas ranger and Arizona rosewood are good candidates for an early fall pruning, if you like a shaped hedge. September is a good time, too, to take drastic measures on an old hedge that has become overgrown at the top.

Geraniums, like tired lawns and tired roses, can be revived as the weather cools. If they are not too far gone, cut them back to produce fresh new growth. If summer has been hard on them, it might be best to dig them up. Resist the temptation to replant the bed with more geraniums; the soil has probably become contaminated with fungus. The farming principle of rotating crops also applies to the home gardener.

Pests and Problems

Good weather for plants and humans is good weather for insects. There's a stirring of white grubs and cutworms in the soil. Pick these out as you dig the ground in preparation for the fall planting. You'll enjoy digging if you start early in the morning while it's cool. Much of the pleasure will be your anticipation of enjoying the fresh flavors of your own winter vegetables.

Expect a resurgence of plant pests toward the end of the month. Dichondra lawns become infested with flea beetles that scar the leaves and weaken the plant to the point of death; treat as directed on page 60. Orange dog caterpillars appear on citrus again. Grape-leaf skeletonizers are back. Shake the vines in the cool of an early morning and many of these pests will fall to the ground. If you should come back from vacation and discover the skeletonizers have completely eaten all the leaves on your grapes, don't try to coax it to grow back now. If you do, the plant will use up next spring's buds and next spring's energy prematurely. Just let it go into an early dry dormancy. This will give the plant a long rest, making it stronger in the spring.

After a good rain, you might see mud tunnels—a result of termite activity. These elaborate constructions cover the dead stalks of desert plants that dried out during the summer. They also climb the stalks of roses, palm trees and saguaros, and lace the walls of buildings. Don't panic; these termites don't attack living plants. Neither do they like bright sunshine, dry desert air or being eaten by birds. That's why they make tunnels to hide and shelter them. By the time you notice termite activity, the insects usually have gone back to their homes deep in the soil and the tunnels will be empty. If you see tunnels against the foundation or sides of your house, brush them off. There's little point in spraying either the tunnels or the surrounding area. The desert is full of termites, and they will surface again when the soil is warm and moist. Watch your house foundations, though; brush, brush!

Harvester Ants

The fall gives us good reason to use transplants in preference to direct sowing. Harvester ants are busy while the soil is warm enough for plant growth. They "go to ground" after the soil has cooled, but if we delay sowing on their account, we lose valuable growing time. Our growing seasons are short. We don't want to be held back by harvester ants. Your trays of seedlings—begun in late August and continued through September—will be safe on a bench, high up from the ants.

Black and Yellow Swallowtail

Keep a sharp look out for a handsome, fluttering butterfly, the black and yellow swallowtail. Don't give it the benefit of a doubt. Its looks are beautiful and its antics are amusing, but it is not showing off or trying to be clever. She is flying around looking for a citrus leaf on which to lay her eggs. They are the size of a pinhead and sit singly on the upper surface of a leaf. The eggs are easy to spot once you know what to look for. If they are not eaten by wasps or other predators, the eggs hatch in a few days into 1/4-inch, brownish caterpillars that start eating immediately. They prefer soft, pale-colored leaves and they can do a lot of damage in a short time.

When the caterpillars become larger, they camouflage themselves by becoming a surprisingly good imitation of a bird dropping. This

Ants become active as temperatures cool. At night leafcutter ants cut leaves off plants and carry the pieces to their homes in the ground, usually finishing the job before daybreak. Protect your plants and seedlings with an insecticide spray.

trick of nature is not designed to fool humans as much as it is to avoid attention from birds. In addition, to make sure nothing bothers it too much, it can shake its head and produce a pair of orange horns. It also gives out a nasty smell when it is stabbed or squeezed. Pick off and destroy these pests.

Grasshoppers

Grasshoppers do their final feeding this month and you may see some pretty big specimens in the fall. Some of these will lay eggs in the soil to produce next spring's generation. Others will find a cozy place to spend the winter and lay their eggs in the spring after they come out. In either case, they are eating your greenery and should be squashed when you see them. Some years you will see lots of little green grasshoppers about 1/2 inch long on your newly planted seedlings. These are the last hatchings of the year and are voracious feeders. Spray them with Malathion 50® or diazinon because these little creatures are usually too active and tiny to catch.

The larger grasshoppers are easy to catch and destroy. Early in the morning when it's cold, they are sluggish and often perch prominently on the sunny top of a plant to get warm.

Cutworms and White Grubs

Be alert for cutworms. These caterpillars live in the soil during the day and assume the soil's color, so it's not always easy to see them. At night, they come out and crawl over the surface, looking for stems. They grasp them tightly with their bodies to get leverage then chew through the stems at ground level. Plants fall over as if beavers have been at work. In the evening spray the soil surface with Malathion 50®, diazinon or Sevin® to control. Read and follow all label directions.

Don't confuse cutworms with white grubs, which are also a nuisance. They stay underground to eat the roots of seedlings. Both can be controlled by spraying the bed with diazinon, Malathion 50® or

Below left: Some caterpillars are hard to find because they align themselves along the stalks. In addition, they are the same green color as the leaves they've eaten!

Below: The orange dog caterpillar looks like a bird dropping, which saves it from being eaten by birds. Pick them off citrus trees and throw them away.

September
In Your Garden

Sevin®. Get the chemical 1 inch deep into the soil where the insects are hiding. If you find white grubs while digging, pick them up and squash them. (White grubs don't breed—they are the larval stage of a beetle.)

Cabbage Loopers

Cabbage loopers are harder to find. They are the exact color of the plant they are feeding on and align themselves along the leaf stalks when they rest. You need good eyesight and patience to discover them before they do a lot of damage to small leaves of seedlings. As soon as you see pieces missing from leaves, make a thorough inspection of the seedling tray or the vegetable bed to find and remove these creatures. Keep this mind when shopping for plants at the nursery, and inspect plants and packs well. Do not buy seedlings with misshapen or chewed leaves.

Grey Aphids

Grey aphids start up at the end of September and stay with us through the winter. They begin in a small cluster, generally under a leaf of cabbage, broccoli, cauliflower, radish or turnip. They suck the juices out of the leaf, deforming it into a pucker, which gives additional coverage and protection to the insects. Although the pucker is on the underside of the leaf, the upper side shows a dull, yellow spot. This is the sign you should recognize. Look underneath and rub out the colony between your finger and thumb. Don't delay and allow the colony to build up. A large number of them will weaken a young plant and make an older one inedible. A spray of 50-50 rubbing alcohol and water solution will kill them. As with cabbage loopers, examine nursery plants carefully before purchase.

Agave Snout-Nosed Weevil

Agave snout-nosed weevils become active again with the return of cooler weather, invading agaves. They prefer older plants, which may be sweeter due to accumulated nutrients. Before they strike, apply diazinon on the top of each agave plant, letting the liquid slowly trickle down to the leaf bases and, finally, to the soil. Follow all label directions. This is a preventive, hit-and-miss measure but worth the effort. If you wait until you see signs of damage it will be too late for treatment. If you discover a completely wilted plant, pull it up. Dispose of it, along with all the beetles and their grubs. Don't leave them in your landscape or they will infest other plants.

Split Fruit of Citrus and Pomegranates

September's storms, coupled with frequent irrigations, can cause citrus fruits to absorb water and expand quickly. The insides swell, but the rigid, outer skin doesn't expand at the same rate. Something has to give. Because the skin has been baked hard by summer sun, exposed fruit often splits. This is particularly true of navel oranges, sweet oranges and tangerines. It's not as serious a problem with grapefruits or lemons. To avoid attracting vinegar beetles, sour-fruit beetles and leaf-footed plant bugs, remove and discard all damaged fruit from trees and from the ground underneath trees. Being careful with watering helps avoid the problem. Turn off the automatic system and use your soil probe to apply the correct amount.

The citrus fruit is nowhere near ripeness in September. If you think it is edible, simply take a bite into the flesh and you'll quickly change your opinion.

How do you tell when pomegranates are ripe? To some extent the skin color is an indication, but not a very reliable one. Some varieties are pale-colored when ripe, while others are almost purple inside and out. The only way to tell is a taste test. Take fruits from the tree and cut them open and sample them.

✓ Special Considerations

Budding on Citrus Trees

Take advantage of fall growth in citrus and do some *budding*. Budding is adding new and different citrus wood, or stock, to an existing tree. If the budding is a success, the stock will grow and produce fruit of the new variety.

A number of experienced gardeners say fall budding is usually more successful than budding in the spring when mild weather can quickly turn to hot summer and dry out the new shoots. The spurt of growth stimulated by the cooling weather is sustained by vigorous sap flow up from the roots to the leaves. If there is plenty of moisture in the soil, this causes the thin bark on the twigs to "slip," or open up easily when it is cut with a sharp knife.

For example, you may have a lemon tree that produces abundantly. You'd like to have a few oranges and grapefruit as well. Just as the first fall buds begin to swell and before the leaves open or flower buds break, make some opening cuts on twigs when the greenish bark is beginning to turn tan. They'll be a bit thicker than a pencil and the bark can be cut easily with a sharp knife.

Into the slit on the twig, insert a freshly cut bud from a high-quality orange or grapefruit tree. Push it downwards so it slides tightly against the inside of the bark. When snug, wrap it up with a length of soft plastic tape to keep the bud from drying out. Keep the tree well supplied with water to sustain new growth; your buds will be part of that new growth. Watch them carefully and as they begin to swell, make a long cut in the plastic wrap to the side of the bud. This opens the plastic and allow the tender bud to grow without obstruction.

Work in several more buds than you think you'll need because not every one will "take." The time available for budding is limited and you won't have another chance until spring. The newly budded shoots will be vulnerable to winter's cold, so protect them carefully on freezing nights.

September
In Your Garden

October

*O*ctober is one of the best months to work in the garden or landscape. The heat of summer has gone, but the cold of winter hasn't arrived. September's plantings and sowings are growing rapidly, but we know they will slow down in November. Last month's gardening rush is over, but a few things still remain to be done before the quiet of winter. The days grow shorter and cooler—mid-eighties are the rule—but the sun is bright. Night temperatures in the fifties give plants a welcome respite from summer stress. This difference between day and night temperatures widens as the month progresses, encouraging those plants that survived the rigors of summer to grow again. If a shower or two washes the dust off our plants, the whole landscape looks fresh and bright. It's ready for another growth spell before cold weather arrives in early December.

October is the month when older leaves on trees and shrubs turn yellow and drop. It's a normal occurrence, almost like a rehearsal for the real fall that's coming. Leaf fall is the chief way trees get rid of unwanted chemicals. Don't worry when you see this for the first time, although it does seem strange that the mild weather that causes new growth also causes your plants to drop colorful leaves.

Weather-worn summer vegetables such as tomatoes, eggplant and bell peppers come to life again. We do not want our citrus and other cold-tender plants to put on new, tender growth this month, although conditions are favorable for them to do so. Experienced gardeners look down the road and know that freezing temperatures are sure to come. Plants that have a lot of new growth on them are more susceptible to frost damage than those with older, more hardened wood.

And October is typically a "buggy" month, so be prepared for pests!

❧ Featured Plants for October

Chinese pole beans continue their prolific ways, producing numerous pods in October. Harvest them often and when they are young as shown for best flavor.

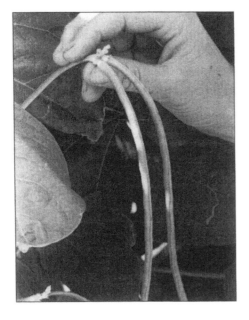

Grapes

Grapes may sometimes begin a fresh flowering and occasionally you get a light crop. Treat grapevines as you do citrus—coax them into dormancy by reducing irrigations. If rain continues to fall in generous amounts, it's unfortunate that grapevines keep growing: The tender growth will be susceptible to cold damage.

Winter Vegetables—Harvest Time

October is a satisfying month because the first harvest of winter vegetables is near. Bush beans sown in August are starting to yield. Lettuce can be picked. Radishes are being eaten, as are Oriental vegetables. There's still lots of life in the Chinese pole beans and black-eyed peas. Everything in the garden is lovely and the future holds bright prospects.

Mushrooms

One kind of growth in the garden that alarms some people is mushrooms. "Where do they come from?" "I didn't have any last year—I've never seen them before." Others sometimes want to know whether one can eat them.

Soil mix is often made from forest products such as fir bark and composted sawdust. When you buy it, you invariably buy other parts of the forest, namely mushroom spores. These "hatch" when moisture and temperatures are favorable to give us brightly colored clusters of miniature mushrooms. They last only a short time. Some people think they are nice—others prefer to avoid them. Mushrooms are simply living on the organic material in the soil mix.

It's difficult to offer advice on whether to eat mushrooms that appear in your landscape. Most are edible, even if they look horrible, but mushroom poisoning is a nasty experience. Books tell us the poisons don't work immediately. By the time you are desperately ill a few days later, you have forgotten exactly which mushroom you made into a gourmet meal.

Don't experiment with mushrooms; go strictly by experience. If you positively recognize a particular kind that you have eaten before, go ahead and enjoy it. If you have no experience, use someone else's—but don't get it over the telephone. Ask them to share a meal of mushrooms with you!

Tomatoes

Once again, tomatoes begin to flower and set fruit, as do eggplant and peppers. August-sown sweet corn is almost ready to harvest and later sowings in September look promising for a Thanksgiving feast. Outdoor tomato plants will do well in the next few weeks, but be ready for the inevitable killing frost. It will result in buckets of green tomatoes. Be prepared. Select recipes ahead of time and use them in pies, relishes, chutneys and jams.

Chinese Pole Beans

Chinese pole beans continue to produce dozens of pods each day. It's a mistake to neglect picking them because the pods become hard rather quickly if left on the vine.

Citrus

A mild fall season, suggesting that winter will also be mild, gives us reason to worry a little about our citrus trees. Because of mild temperatures and shortening days, our trees put on a spurt of growth. Warm October rains also stimulate growth in citrus trees, sometimes to the extent that they produce flowers. Most flowers fall off, but sometimes they develop into those out-of-season, maverick fruit that surprise us late next summer. There's nothing we can do about winter rains and we like to have them. But we must manage our citrus trees carefully this month. Don't irrigate them if the soil is moist. Let the rains determine how much they will grow, and hope for the best.

This new growth might encourage beginning gardeners to invoke one of the cardinal rules regarding fertilizer applications—namely, support new growth when it occurs by applying a nitrogen fertilizer. Normally this makes good sense, but at the end of the year when the next few weeks are sure to bring freezing nights, we don't want to encourage or assist new growth. Don't be tempted to help it along. Remember, new growth is frost tender so do not fertilize again until February.

Watch the condition of the new growth carefully and allow it to wilt just a little before you water again. As the month progresses, try for intervals of 20 days between irrigations. When the first frost of the year strikes, and it usually surprises us in mid-November, you'll be glad you were tough-minded in October.

Plants in Containers—Move to Sunshine

Here's a light chore to do after shadow and shade patterns have changed and the strength has gone out of the sun's heat. These are cues to move plants in containers into sunnier locations. Five-gallon-size are easy enough to move, but half-barrels can be a struggle. If they are on a concrete patio, try slipping short pieces of iron pipe under them and roll them to the new spot. If on grass or bare soil, get some friends to help you. Give the containers a quarter turn about every month so plant growth is even. Left in the same position, plants become leggy, reaching for the sunlight.

Black-plastic containers gather the sun's heat—desirable in winter—and plant roots thrive in the warm soil. It's a good way to extend the harvests of peppers, tomatoes and eggplant. Some gardeners even dig up such plants, trim the branches a bit and put them into black 5-gallon buckets for growing in a sheltered, sunny place. When frost threatens, they cover the plants with a sheet or bring them inside for the night.

Plant your winter garden, or some of it, in containers. If you were unable to get things going last month, October plantings will catch up in growth because of the additional warmth of the container soil.

Pecan Trees

Maintain an irrigation schedule with pecan trees in spite of the coming cold weather. Nuts must continue to get regular water so they fill out

If you are growing plants in pots, move them to a sunny spot and watch them grow faster than plants in a shady, cold part of your yard.

well, otherwise there will be a number of shriveled nuts instead of plump ones. If the trees are deprived of water for too long, expect a premature nut fall.

It's normal to have some nuts drop from your pecan tree. The first time you experience an October shedding of immature nuts you assume that something awful has happened. The ground seems covered with black nuts and it's happening just before harvest! Look up into the tree; you'll most likely see as many nuts still on the tree as on the ground, if not more. The nuts on the tree are as green as the leaves; those are the good ones. Those on the ground are the poorly filled ones; they're no good to the tree, so it drops them. To make sure the good nuts stay where they are and continue to fatten, give your pecan trees one last deep irrigation before harvest.

A number of beginning gardeners mistakenly view this nutfall as a sign that the crop is ready for picking. They start knocking the remaining nuts off the tree at a time when they should remain in order to fill out. In any event, it's usually best to harvest pecans from the ground. Let the fat nuts drop when they are ready.

🌱 Planting

There's still time to plant most trees and shrubs. Junipers and pine trees, for example, will grow new roots for several more weeks, even if air temperatures cool considerably. Desert trees and shrubs, as well as hardy cacti, can also be planted.

It's risky to plant citrus trees because damaging freezes are likely to occur in November and December. Although the soil is warm enough to encourage root growth and begin establishment, it's safer to plant deciduous fruit trees now. You could have planted citrus trees in early September, but better wait now until March.

Beware Continuous Cropping

Native desert soils are typically free of harmful bacteria and fungi. When we grow annual plants, whether bedding plants or vegetables, in the same soil year after year (and provide regular amounts of moisture) we provide food for these harmful organisms. The longer we grow such plants, the more the organisms multiply and the weaker our plants become. The organisms are now soil pests. And they are killers.

Care of the soil is part of good husbandry. It's best done by growing different plants each year in the same plot of ground. Sometimes the soil has to lie fallow in an effort to starve out a disease. Crop rotation—resting the soil from continuous cropping with one kind of plant—makes a lot of sense. It's hard to get rid of soil diseases. And they can make a once-valuable garden plot worthless.

October is the month to pull out the remnants of weakened, past-prime summer flowers and put in cool-season flowers. Flowers pull fertility from the soil just like any farm crop, so it's best to renew the soil's fertility by adding organic matter, ammonium phosphate and sulphur each time you plant afresh. It's also a good idea to rotate your color crops by planting different kinds of flowers.

Give new transplants plenty of moisture while their roots are getting

Digging holes for tree planting is best left to the cooler weeks. If you have caliche you must get through it if you want your tree to flourish.

established. October's days are sunny, suggesting a need for frequent watering, but as temperatures cool, plants' needs for water actually diminish. Use your soil probe to tell you when to irrigate. Don't rely on an automatic sprinkler system. In fact, it's better not to sprinkle flowering plants at all; it discolors the flowers. Flood irrigate or use a drip system.

Nursery Bargains?

Nurseries often are anxious to clear their sales areas this month to make room for Christmas trees and fall gardening materials. There are bargains to be had, but be careful. Inspect plants carefully, especially the roots. If roots are going round and round at the bottom of the container, the plant has been in the container too long. It is no bargain.

October, especially the first half of the month, is a good time to fill your garden with cool-season, leafy vegetables. It's acceptable to plant during the second half of the month, but the cooler soil will cause these plantings to mature more slowly.

Chrysanthemum Color

Nurseries have plenty of chrysanthemums in October. They are inexpensive, and if you buy them at the point of flowering, you'll know what colors you're getting. Use them for beds, in hanging bowls and in containers on the patio. Place splashes of winter color all over the yard, but don't think of chrysanthemums as permanent additions, even though they are perennials. It's hardly worth your while to coddle them through a hot summer. When flowering is over, pull them out and replant with something better adapted to hot weather.

Planting Lawns

Whether you are overseeding Bermudagrass or starting a new rye-grass lawn, the weather will be just right sometime in October. Don't panic. You'll have about three weeks of optimum conditions and several more days when sowing is still possible. But when is the time just right? If you plant too soon, while temperatures remain hot, most rye-grass seed will not germinate. Any that does will be weakened by com-petition from the still-vigorous Bermudagrass. If you wait too long, the seed will germinate slowly due to the cool soil and the Bermudagrass will have gone dormant and started to turn brown. The trick is to have the fresh green of ryegrass seedlings imperceptibly replace the fading green of Bermudagrass.

A soil thermometer comes in handy now. Sow your ryegrass lawn when the soil temperature reaches 75F at 2 inches deep. Don't rely on last year's sowing date, and don't wait for a neighbor to begin his oper-ation. The weather is suitable into mid-November, although the longer you wait the cooler the soil becomes, and this means that seeds will germinate slower.

Planting the Cool-Season Garden

Set out the cool-season vegetable plants that you sowed in August. Dig small planting holes in the garden. Make a starter solution by mixing 1 tablespoon of ammonium phosphate in a gallon of water. Apply a pint of this solution per plant to make a mud pie, and set out the new plants without bending their roots. Space closely and you can eat the first thinning as a tender, gourmet harvest.

Wildflowers

If you want wildflowers in the spring, sow seeds now. Don't lightly scat-ter seeds all over, as does Mother Nature. Instead, select sunny sec-tions of your landscape and dig wandering, snakelike pathways between trees and shrubs. Most wildflowers like sun, not shade. Dig 10 to 12 inches deep, mixing in 2 or 3 inches of steer manure and one pound of ammonium phosphate for every 100 square feet of "pathway."

With the soil prepared, it's time to get rid of the weeds by watering the area so they will germinate. Hoe them out while they are small. Next, prepare the area to sow the wildflower seeds. Rake the soil in one direction, making shallow trenches that will serve as miniature fur-rows. Sow the wildflower seed thickly, then cross-rake to bury the seed. Seed should be planted less than 1 inch deep.

The best wildflower seeds are those that you collected from your garden last spring before the winds scattered them. If you buy seeds, select a "Southwest desert" mixture, or select individual wildflowers that are native to your desert region.

Sprinkle the area daily until the seedlings emerge. Don't wait too long to cover them with chicken wire to keep out the birds. Extend time between waterings as the seedlings grow or if rainfall is abundant. Pull out the weed seedlings as you see them, and thin the wildflowers if they are too thick. (You can transplant many wildflower seedlings if the days are moist and cool.)

Perennial wildflowers such as desert mallow may show new clumping growth this month. Cut back the old stalks. If rainfall is scant or nonexistent, water plants well.

Bulb-Planting Time

October is the month for planting bulbs. A number of bulbs are suitable for the desert, most which originate from Africa. You can enjoy a little success with many of the Dutch bulbs, too, but not hyacinths or tulips. Several kinds of bulbs can be left in the ground all through the hot summer. They will survive provided they are allowed to remain dry. As soon as the first winter rains fall, you'll see leaf shoots of amaryllis, daffodil, narcissus, jonquil, Star-of-Bethlehem and leucojum. This is your signal to start watering them to keep them growing. Bulbs should be divided and thinned out after a couple of years. Otherwise they crowd one another and the competition causes them to produce small blooms.

Don't follow traditional bulb-planting depth charts. Most originate in Europe, where it's wise to put bulbs deep in the soil to keep them safe from the cold. Plant daffodils 8 inches deep in the desert and they emerge and flower about the time the weather is hot. As a result, the blooms last for only a short time. Your goal is for your bulbs to flower before March, so plant them at one-half the traditional recommended depth.

Dig the planting ground deeply and add in ammonium phosphate— or bone meal, if you are an old-time bulb gardener. Avoid adding lots of organic matter, which holds moisture. Bulbs will rot if they are kept too moist. Some gardeners plant bulbs on a 2-inch layer of coarse sand to ensure good drainage. Then they fill in the soil on top of the bulb. Don't forget: the point goes up; the flat part goes down. In the case of ranunculus, the "fingers" point down.

Bulbs are succulent and live "off their hump" when they start their growth. Don't drown them with frequent irrigations. Don't let them dry out, either, once they have started growing.

If you plant daffodil bulbs between yourself and the sun, you will only see their backs; daffodils always face the sun. You'll get a better result if you plant them so that your back is to the sun so their flowers will face toward you.

The Temptation of Azaleas

As soon as the weather begins to cool, there's usually a fine display of azaleas, camellias and gardenias in the nurseries. They look lovely in their gallon containers. Shiny leaves and full buds seem to call out for you to buy them. Don't fall for it. These plants have just come from cooler, more humid, less sunny places. They are growing in a soil mix high in acidic peat moss. Such plants seldom last a year in the desert.

October is strawberry planting time—if you can find healthy plants that have come through a hard summer. They'll grow well in the cooler air and soil until December, when you cover the bed with a tent of clear plastic to keep them growing. Pick fruit in March, April and May.

Plant them out now and they'll do fine until June or July; then they'll begin to drop their leaves and die back. If they do survive a summer, perhaps in the shade of a north wall, their buds drop before they open. You have to be a special kind of gardener to be successful with these plants in the desert.

Strawberries

You may not be able to buy strawberry plants in October at the nurseries and they will be expensive if you can find them. If you are lucky enough to have extra new plants from your own bed because everything went well during the summer—which it usually doesn't—you'll be able to plant up economically.

From now on the weather will be kind to strawberries—even through winter—and you'll have strong plants on the point of flowering when spring weather returns. People who put out strawberries in the spring lose this head start. Their plants produce only a few berries before hot weather stresses them. Take advantage of fall's good growing weather and a week or two after planting, irrigate strawberries with a little houseplant food in the water.

Fava Beans, Lettuce and Radishes

Fava beans are a favorite of Italian gardeners, and others, too. They are also called broad beans, horse beans or Italian beans. You may not find seed in local nurseries, so you'll have to order them from a catalog.

You may find dried fava beans in gourmet food stores. Buy a small amount and try them out for taste although they are best when freshly harvested and eaten as shelled beans. Dried beans can be ground into a tasty flour for flavoring soups and breads. The small, round ones don't grow as well as the larger flat kinds. Among the larger kinds it seems that any variety does as well as another.

Although fava beans are legumes and improve the soil through their root bacteria, they won't do well in poor soil. Sow the large seeds 1 inch deep. There's no need to soak them, even though they are hard. Keep the soil moist.

Fava beans grow into woody plants about 4 feet high and send out basal shoots, so give them plenty of room. Unlike most members of the bean family, they are pollinated by insects. Therefore, it's a good idea to have a block of flowering plants rather than long thin rows, the same as with corn. Sow seed every 18 inches on the square. If you don't have a lot of garden space, interplant with Bibb lettuce or radishes. These will be harvested before the fava beans become tall and crowded. The beans are slow growers in the early stages.

Deciduous Fruit Trees

More and more gardeners are realizing that fall is an excellent time to plant deciduous fruit trees, even though they are about to drop their leaves and go dormant.

Desert winters are seldom severe enough to freeze the ground. It is the cool temperature of the air that we notice and this is what affects our garden plants. The soil actually stays warm enough to allow tree roots to continue growing. The cooling air and shortening days cause the leaves to slow down and drop off. The top part of the tree doesn't lose any moisture. Conditions are entirely favorable.

◖ Watering

October can be a rainy month and we know moisture from rain is much more effective than irrigations from the hose. Rain helps get plants established. Those planted a few days ago don't go into shock and are stimulated to grow. If you have any late planting to do, it's fun

Insect pests typically arrive with the cooling weather. This prickly pear is not diseased but invaded by cochineal scale, an insect that protects itself with a waxy covering. Even insecticides are repelled by it. The best control method is to blast the insects off with a strong jet of water. Squeeze the insects and you get a strong red color that can be used as a dye.

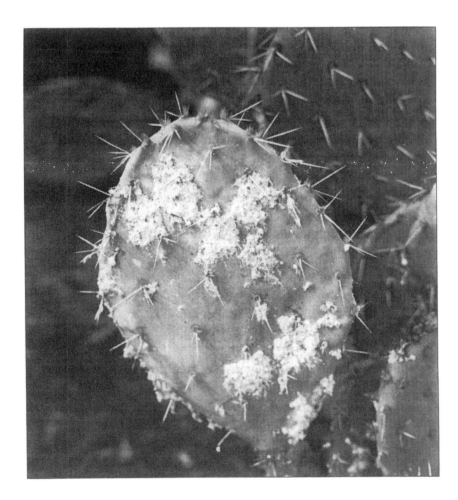

to set plants into moist soil, even during a shower. We are almost guaranteed success. It's the same with seeds—they come up more readily. In addition, the increased humidity favors plant growth.

Semitropical fruit trees need protection from future cold. Deciduous trees need more cold than they usually get in the desert. This contradictory state of affairs can be resolved in both cases by withholding irrigations even though continued fall showers interfere. A wet fall gives us a true desert dilemma. As temperatures continue to drop, plant growth begins to slow. And here is the dilemma. We want our fruit trees to rest, but we also want our winter vegetables, flowers and landscape shrubs to continue to grow.

Pruning

Don't do heavy pruning in October. A pruning cut stimulates tender new growth, and you don't want that now. Limbs and heavy branches of trees should not be trimmed except to repair storm damage. You want to keep the tree calm.

Hedges are another story. The vigorous new shoots produced by September pruning can now be lightly sheared. The first half of October is a good time to thicken up a hedge with frequent trims.

Pests and Problems

Cochineal Scale

It looks like small clumps of wetted toilet paper on prickly pear pads. If you don't do anything about it, your plants will be weakened for a long time; they might even die. "It" is a colony of cochineal scale insects. Centuries ago, colonies were collected from wild prickly pear plants in the Mediterranean region, as they are in Mexico today, for use as a dye. If you're not interested in making your own dye, the best way to get rid of a colony is to blast it off with a strong jet of water. The scale's protective fuzz keeps insecticides from its soft body, making chemical spraying largely ineffective. However, a spray of 50-50 rubbing alcohol and water will dissolve the fuzz, killing the pests.

Cutworms

Your morning inspections may discover a few seedlings lying on their sides, with a neatly nibbled stem. This is the work of cutworms. In early evening, spray the soil surface with diazinon or Malathion 50®. When cutworms come up for their nightly feed, they will be killed by the poison.

If you don't want to use chemical controls, wrap kitchen foil around the stem of each seeding—a tiresome task. Or place a gallon glass jar over each plant and push it partially down into the soil. This will keep the pest away from the plant stem and also provide a mini-greenhouse to protect the plant from the cold. Remove during the day if temperatures are warm.

Aphids

In October, aphids get a second chance. They are opportunistic and destructive, feeding on new growth encouraged by the mild October weather. There may be a repeat of springtime populations—green, brown and black aphids—but they are sure to be joined by grey aphids. You find these especially like cabbage-family plants.

Inspect young plants closely and often. Rub out the first pest invasions. A spray of 50-50 solution of rubbing alcohol and water will control them. Once they get established, there's little to be done except serve the vegetable with a lot of cheese sauce!

Harvester Ants

Harvester ants remain troublesome this month. They work furiously, gathering green leaves to store for the winter. Active at night, they easily strip plants and young seedlings before dawn. Find them with a flashlight and you'll be amazed at the intense activity that will be over by daylight. They leave behind a telltale trail of small pieces of leaves and maybe a few stragglers in the early morning, making it easy for you to discover their nest.

The next night, while all the ants are out cutting and stealing your plants, pour diazinon or Amdrol® pellets down the hole. The ants' compelling instinct to carry something home forces them to track the poison deep inside their nest.

Grasshoppers

Grasshoppers have a destructive last fling before the frost. October mornings are cool and insects, being cold-blooded, are sluggish. They are easy to catch and dispose of during the first few hours of the day. Left alone, grasshoppers will lay eggs that overwinter in the soil and hatch out next spring. Sometimes grasshoppers, though old and fat, will survive a mild winter. We should all hope for a chilly November and December to kill off a number of these kinds of pests.

Gophers

Gophers spend the summer *aestivating.* This is a word similar in meaning to hibernating, but it refers to inactivity during the hot time of the year. Who can blame a gopher for doing this?

Below: One of nature's beneficial predators par-excellence, the praying mantis. Keep these.

Below right: But the katydid grasshopper is a pest. Destroy these!

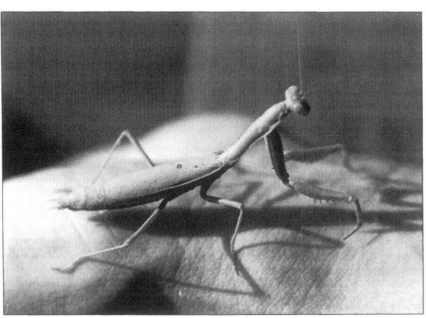

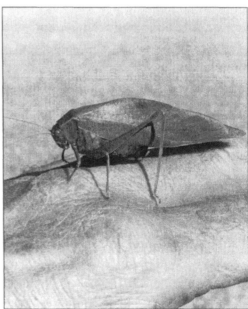

However, we put a lot of blame on gophers that come out of this resting period. October's mild weather gives them a lot of energy to tunnel all over the place, bury our new plantings and eat the roots of tomato and pepper plants that have likewise recovered from summer's heat.

It's not effective to put out poisoned grain, hoping the gopher will eat it. It's a dangerous and irresponsible thing to do. You might poison a pet, some birds or perhaps a curious child might eat the colored grain. It's not effective to drown them out by leaving a hose running in a tunnel. You simply waste water because it flows out the other end of the tunnel. The tunnels can be quite long and the gopher—if it is washed out of its passageway—runs off, out of sight.

Some people try to gas the animals by sealing all the holes but one. Then they attach a hose from it to their car's exhaust. This might work—as might "gopher bombs" you buy in nurseries—but you never know.

You can protect your plants in gopher country by wrapping the roots in chicken wire. Dig large planting holes and line them with a box of 1-inch mesh chicken wire. Of course any roots that grow through the mesh will be at risk. And sometimes the gopher tunnels his way into the wire cage and feasts on roots at his leisure.

Other animals eat gophers. If you don't like to have snakes, owls, hawks and coyotes living with you, then get a cat—but don't overfeed it to the point of fatness and laziness. A motivated cat makes a great gopher hunter.

Two interesting tricks might be effective. One, buy or make an animated windmill device on top of a pole that you stick in the ground. The vibrations of the windmill, especially if you incorporate a little man beating on an anvil, are carried to the ground through the pole. The gophers think an earthquake is taking place and they scamper off! At least that's what the salesperson tells us. But the salesperson can't tell us what to do when the wind stops blowing!

Below left: Insects aren't the only pests that reappear with cooler weather. Plant-eating pocket gophers become a nuisance again. Trap them in their tunnels, called runs.

Below: A rabbit's eye view of a well-protected vegetable garden. Screening off the garden is the only way to keep them from eating your harvest.

October
In Your Garden

Two, surround your garden with a planting of castor beans. It is said that their roots are a deterrent to gophers. But castor beans are a summertime plant and gophers are more active when it is cool. Some gardeners say this doesn't matter because the roots send out their smell even when dead. Other skeptical people think such gardeners pour castor oil down the tunnels when no one is looking.

The most effective way to control gophers is to use gopher traps. (Rat traps seldom work.) Garden and hardware stores sell these traps. Ask the salesperson to show you how to set them. Wear gloves when handling traps to avoid leaving your scent. Use these traps with caution around children. Buy at least two traps, because you don't know which way the animal is traveling along its tunnel. Set one trap pointing one way and the second pointing the other. Select an active run (tunnel) identified by a fresh heap of dirt the gopher has pushed up. Exclude daylight from the disturbed soil with a board or rock or fill the hole with dirt. Inspect daily and dispose of the bodies.

Rabbits

Your garden and landscape plants are full of moisture. That's why cottontail rabbits go for them. For this reason they are another pest of the month—or most of the year if you live on the outskirts of town. Misguided people who feed them call them *bunnies*.

It's useless putting out blood meal, moth balls, pepper, hair from the barber shop, or chemical deterrents. They last for a day or two in the dry desert air and the wind blows them away. Coyotes and birds of prey eat rabbits. And so do some cats. But most dogs don't—not even if you tell them to. The only effective thing to do about rabbits is to surround your garden completely with fencing. Buy it at least 3 feet wide with small mesh. Bury it 6 inches deep so the varmints can't squeeze under it. And don't ever leave the gate open!

Citrus Fruit Split

Navel oranges readily split at this time. The inside swells quickly but the skin can't expand. After a hot, dry summer, it has grown tough and rigid. Split fruit never recovers. Remove them from the tree because their smell attracts insects that further spoil the fruit by bringing in bacteria. Splitting is worse on trees that were kept dry during summer.

✓ Special Considerations

Time to Encourage Dormancy

"Apply fertilizer when new leaves appear" is a good rule to remember, except in the fall! Be pleased that your plants are growing this month, but don't encourage them. Allow them to slow down in harmony with the gradually cooling weather.

"Harden off" tender plants. In other words, ease your plants into an early dormancy by letting them dry out a little more between irrigations. Of course, don't allow plants to dry so thoroughly that they become stressed or die. Don't water in smaller amounts; you still have to moisten the soil around roots regularly. Instead, lengthen the interval between waterings. Should it rain, a distinct possibility in October, your strategy will be spoiled somewhat, but work on the assumption that it won't rain.

Retain Soil Warmth for Vegetables

As long as the sun shines enough during the day, the soil will be warmed. Your goal is to catch and keep this warmth around your vegetables. Lay plastic sheets on the ground between the plant rows. If you have a lot of weeds—a consequence of fall rains—use black plastic. Otherwise, clear plastic does a better job. Toward the end of the month, create a structure with a clear plastic sheet wrapped over a framework of construction mesh above the bed. This tunnel acts as a temporary greenhouse for little expense. Open up the ends on a hot day to avoid build up of heat, but allow it to remain closed most of the time, retaining moisture and warmth. Keep it in place until spring so plants will continue to grow. A tunnel-shaped structure is particularly useful for strawberries. (See photo, page 138.)

Using a Greenhouse

If you have a greenhouse, this is the month to fill it up with end-of-summer plants, replanted in their 5-gallon buckets. If their foliage is luxuriant, cut back some branches. This keeps the plant in balance because it lost a lot of roots when you dug it up. The pruning will encourage new shoots to grow and, after some time, they will produce flowers. If the greenhouse is kept warm—around 70F day and night—the flowers will turn into fruit.

A greenhouse is a good value during winter months. It's hard on the pocketbook to keep one cool during the desert summer. But in winter you trap the sun's warmth, which costs you nothing provided you keep the doors closed. You'll need a heater during December and January if you grow summertime plants. Tomatoes require night temperatures of about 75F to maintain production. A greenhouse lets you keep harvesting summertime plants, but heating costs will be high.

Wintertime plants such as lettuce, peas and cabbage grow more quickly in a greenhouse than those outside and at little cost of heating because the sun's heat will be enough. Later in winter you can start new plants from seed in the greenhouse to prepare for spring.

Annual Weeds

Late October is usually a time of cooler temperatures and rainfall. These conditions favor seed germination for both weeds and wildflowers. Eliminate weeds with a sharp Dutch hoe. Work the flat blade back and forth just one inch deep into the soil when weeds are young and easy to remove. Once weeds get more than a few inches tall, you'll have to dig or pull them out.

November

*T*he cooling weather is an obvious sign that the long summer is coming to an end. Days are shorter, the sun is lower in the sky, and shadows, even at midday, are longer. There might be a few hot days at the beginning of the month, but the danger in November is that the first freeze of the season will take you—and your plants—by surprise before the month's end. Deciduous trees will be dropping their leaves soon so it's time to think compost. Create the frame or clear an area to hold the materials.

We can't do much about the summertime vegetables except perhaps dig them up and preserve them in containers placed in a sheltered environment through winter. If they survive as vigorous plants, they can be planted out again in the spring.

Start recording the night tempera-tures, using a minimum thermome-ter. It will record how cold it got last night. Chart temperatures and com-pare with the official forecast and the actual record at the airport.
You'll be better able to act on forecasts if you know if you are in a warmer or a colder part of town.

🌱 Featured Plants for November

Landscape Plants

Cool-season flowers and ryegrass lawns continue to grow in November, but native vegetation and warm-season plants slow considerably. Deciduous trees and shrubs begin to turn color, a sign of beginning dormancy, and more yellow leaves drop each day. The first frost takes care of the rest. Evergreens such as bougainvillea and citrus will hang on to their leaves, but as they go dormant they show a lot of pale green or yellow. Don't worry; this is normal. The leaves will green up when warmer temperatures return.

Citrus—Time for Taste Test

You'll notice a color change in citrus fruits at the beginning of November, too. This is not a sign that the fruit is ripe (although tanger-ines, navel oranges and lemons may be ready to enjoy), but that cooler temperatures are affecting the pigment in their rinds. Don't go by the rind color alone. But the question remains, how do you tell when your fruit is ready to eat? A simple taste test does the trick: Find a friend, give him a fruit to eat, and watch. If his lips pucker up, you have to wait a few days more; if a smile covers his face, then go for the harvest!

Tangerines are the first to be ready, then navel oranges followed by tangelos. Limes and lemons ripen in November, but they stay green until later in the year. Sweet oranges won't be ready until March. Grapefruits, although yellow in November, won't be at their best until April or May.

Citrus picking is not like harvesting apples. Pick just what you need and leave the rest on the tree for another day. The tree is the best place to store citrus fruit. (But tangerines need to be eaten during the next five or six weeks, so don't hold back once this fruit is ready to eat.)

Pecans

Pecans begin to fall off the tree, but don't get too excited. The first nut-falls are generally poor quality, such as those that are not fully filled or are damaged by insects. Wait for the main crop, which is still on the tree. Don't climb up pecan trees to knock off the nuts. Wait for the ripe nuts to fall off on their own and pick them from the ground.

The first frost of the year will cause a lot of nuts to drop. The freeze won't hurt them, and they will be nuts that are nicely filled. Don't be in a hurry to eat them, either. Green nuts have the same effect on your stomach as green apples.

Asparagus

Asparagus plants begin to look a little weary in November. Some years this does not occur until cold weather comes on or it coincides with the same sharp frost that knocks nuts off the pecan trees. Asparagus plants have grown satisfactorily all through the summer in full sun. Now it's their turn to rest.

As soon as asparagus leaves begin to turn brown, stop watering. Dormancy can be induced by allowing plants to dry. They will benefit because they need the rest. Cut off all leaves, right down to the ground. Be sure the plants are dormant, otherwise the trimming will act as a pruning and cause fresh growth. You don't want new growth until spring. This is important! If it seems the plants are not quite dormant, don't risk cutting them back. Let the bed stay dry. Withhold nutrients until spring just in case we have a wet winter.

Lawns

Be sure your ryegrass lawn is dry when you mow it. Otherwise, the machine's wheels will crush the soft, tender, new leaves and invite disease organisms to enter the watery tissues. Sometimes, particularly if the mower blades are dull, young seedlings are torn out of the ground. Use a catcher to gather the soft clippings; they make good compost. If you leave them lying around they provide a home for diseases as they lay on wet turf. If you want your winter lawn to look great, be sure your mower blades are sharp and adjusted.

Desert Broom

The desert broom is a much maligned plant. It grows so successfully on its own that it's considered a weed. Admittedly, it sometimes grows where it is not wanted from seed blown in by the wind, and it's not easy to kill with chemicals. It's hard to dig out, too, because its roots are strong and deep. Still, it's a green plant all through the heat of the summer and requires hardly any irrigation. It makes a fine specimen plant standing alone, or it can be planted to make a hedge. Trim it to make it tidy. During growth periods in the spring, give it a cup of ammonium sulphate and water well.

In November it attracts your attention. Whole female plants are bent over with the weight of tiny white flowers; the bushes appear to be frosted or covered with snow. It's an attractive sight in the fall sunshine. Now comes the criticism. There are some who believe that the white fluff floating in the breeze causes allergies. This is not true. The stuff is too big to get up your nose, so it's impossible to breathe it into your body. Allergies are caused by male plants when they flower in the spring. If you do react to desert broom in the spring, get rid of the

The result of a well-spaced garden, these winter vegetables were thinned to allow for proper growth. They can be kept growing during the cool months by covering them with a temporary greenhouse— a tunnel of clear plastic.

male plants around your yard. (They are the ones that do not produce any white seed plumes.) Be aware, however, that it will take some serious digging to get the roots out.

🌱 Planting

November is not commonly a planting month. It's a month for enjoying the results of work you did in September and October. In lower, warmer elevations you may be able to repair gaps in newly seeded lawns and flowerbeds, and don't forget to dead-head pansies, stock, calendulas, petunias and roses.

Fava Beans and Peas

Peas and fava beans prefer cool soil. If you sow their seeds at the beginning of November, they will germinate if the soil does not remain too moist. They will grow slowly during the winter and then put on a burst of growth early in the spring. This will provide you with a harvest that starts in January and goes through to April. These plants are fairly frost resistant, although early flowers are sometimes damaged by cold. If you let the winter go by and sow their seed in January, you'll get a short harvest, as well as a light one.

Thin Veggie Seedlings

If you have sown lettuce, beets, radishes, cabbage or cauliflower (any of the winter vegetables) directly in the garden, it's time to thin the seedlings before they crowd one another.

In the fall, most gardeners prefer to set out transplants rather than sow seeds. But direct seeding can be successful if soil temperatures are favorable and the young plants get off to a good start. You can lose seedlings to ants and sparrows, but if your September seedlings survived, it's time to thin them. Allowed to compete with one another for too little nutrients and moisture causes them all to be weak, spindly and subject to disease. Give young plants plenty of space.

Don't throw away the thinnings. In fancy restaurants they are considered gourmet sprouts so you might as well eat them at home. Wash them, roots and all, and mix into a salad or side dish.

Watering

Citrus

Continue to give your citrus trees deep irrigations but let the soil surface dry out between waterings. Ripening fruit shouldn't frighten you into frequent irrigations. Obviously, don't let the trees dry out to the point where fruit shrivels and drops off, but the water need of trees is greatly reduced during cool weather. You'll encourage new growth by overirrigating now. It can easily happen if we get a few warm days.

Deciduous Fruit Trees and Grapes

Give these plants the same treatment. Freezing will not hurt them unless they are actively growing, which they shouldn't be. They need a long resting period. The sooner plants begin to rest, the better. Drying out deciduous plants is one way to add to the dormancy usually induced by cold temperatures. In the desert we don't have enough cold. We supplement it with a little dryness and hope it doesn't rain.

Cool-Season Color

If you overwater flowers, and this is easy to do if November is wet and you haven't adjusted the automatic irrigation system, expect soil-borne fungus diseases to kill your plants. You can drench the soil with a fungicide in the early stages of such diseases to save appearances. Try Captan®, Dyrene® or Benomyl®). But it's much better to change the conditions that favor the fungus. Irrigate less often and the soil will not remain wet and cold all the time.

Wildflowers

The wildflower seeds you sowed in October have now turned into a carpet of young plants, provided there have been intermittent rains or you have irrigated regularly. Keep up the water if rains are infrequent. It's helpful to provide the plants with nutrients, too, even if they are desert natives. Scatter half a pound of ammonium nitrate for every 100 square feet of area. Water it in, being sure to wash the fertilizer off the leaves or it will burn them. Do this every three or four weeks to keep plants growing well, but don't overdo it. Fertilize enough so that the foliage is dark green, but not too dark green or you'll delay flowering. Too much nitrogen might suppress flowering altogether.

Fertilizing

If your winter vegetable plants are growing, extend their activity by using small amounts of ammonium nitrate fertilizer. Don't think, however, that you can bring dormant plants back into growth.

Scatter ammonium nitrate on the soil around plants at the rate of half a pound to every 100 square feet. Water it in well, being sure to

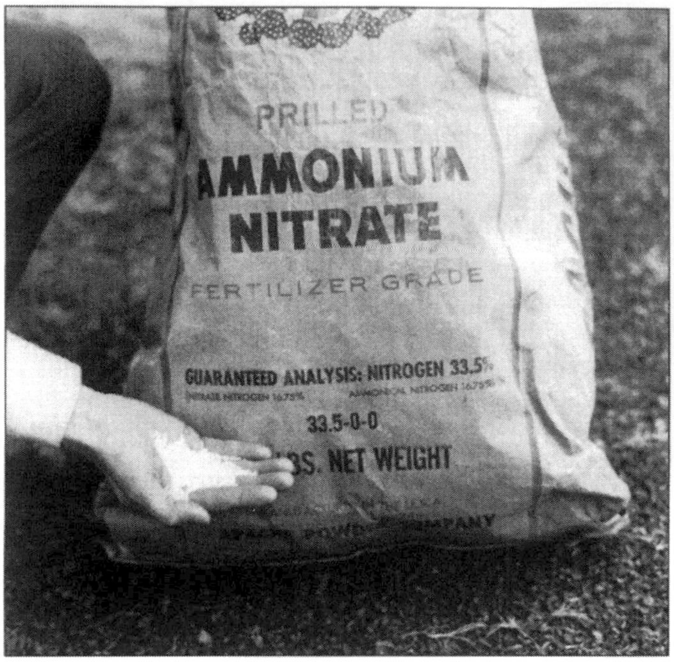

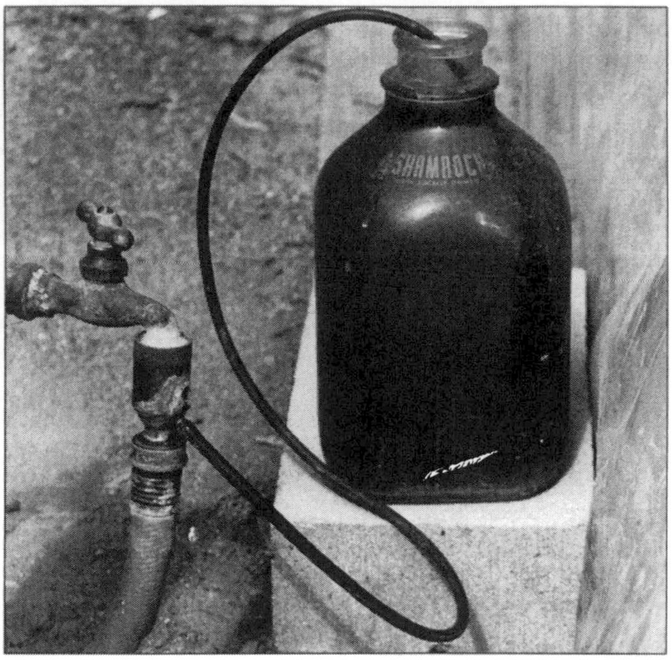

Above: A soluble fertilizer containing nitrate is preferred during the cooler months because it can be used by growing plants. Ammonium sulphate needs warm soil before it becomes available to plants.

Above right: A good way to apply soluble fertilizer to growing plants is to include it with the irrigation. Fertilizer is sucked out of the container through the tube into the flow of water from the faucet.

wash fertilizer off the leaves. If fertilizer is washed into the growing point of a lettuce or cabbage, it will kill the plant.

Another way to apply soluble fertilizer is to put a tablespoon of it into a gallon of water and use this solution to irrigate plants. Better still, put half a cup of ammonium nitrate in a jar and use a hose proportioner to suck it out as you sprinkle the garden. Keep your plants growing, even into cold weather, with such a feeding every 10 days or so.

Ammonium sulphate is the usual garden fertilizer, and it works very well in warm soils, but spread it on a lawn in November and nothing happens. The reason is that bacteria are dormant; they can't change ammonium to nitrate. Try ammonium nitrate. It is stronger than ammonium sulphate, so you use less. Apply about 1 pound to every 100 square feet of winter lawn about every two weeks.

Pruning

November is still too early to prune deciduous trees, whether they are shade trees or fruit trees, even though their leaves may have dropped. Trees should be as close to complete dormancy as possible before pruning. Test for dormancy by checking the moisture content. Snip the end of a twig to see the amount of sap. If you see sap flow, be patient. If cut branches exude sap, the moisture traps and invites invasions by fungi and bacteria, blown about in the wind. Try the twig snap test again in December. However, January or even February may be the best month to prune. See page 7.

Pests and Problems

Birds

A new pest is developing in the desert. Birds are eating (or at least spoiling) our ripening citrus fruit. If the winter is a dry one, it's hard on birds and they turn to whatever sources are available to them. You may not actually see it happen. All you see is a neat hole, as if a child had

Ripening citrus fruits are sweet and birds are thirsty. After birds peck the the fruit, gnats are attracted to the damage. They introduce bacteria that start up a fermentation, which attracts more gnats. The end result is that your fruit is spoiled and it's best to throw it away.

stuck a pencil into the fruit. Out of the hole emerge a lot of tiny flies. Soon the hole turns brown and rots, and the fruit is finished before it's ready to eat. Many people think the small insects, which are called vinegar beetles or fruit flies, make the holes, but that's not the case. They are simply attracted by the smell of damaged ripening fruit. The bacteria they track into the sugary juice turns the juice to vinegar.

Pick off damaged fruit. If the damage has been done recently, you can eat it if you want. Badly damaged fruit should be thrown away. Don't toss it on the ground or it will produce a strong smell, attracting more gnats. Chop them up and add to the compost pile.

Sapsuckers and thrashers make the holes. (They like fruit juice as much as you!) They don't heed such warning devices as scarecrows, rubber snakes or stuffed owls. All you can do is cover the tree with a fine-mesh net. These can be bought at nurseries in varying sizes. Unfortunately, bird nets also catch birds and lizards and they may die if our inspection trips are not frequent enough to notice them. A white sheet might make a better cover if you discover trapped animals become a problem.

Split Citrus Fruit

Pomegranates and oranges split their skins. The smell of the juice attracts insects that carry bacteria on their feet. Soon, a fermentation or rot begins. Pick off all split fruit and put them in the trash can or compost heap. Left lying around they are an attractive nuisance summoning more pests.

✓ Special Considerations

Preserve Heat for Winter Vegetables

We need to take good care of our newly planted winter vegetables. They must be kept growing.

This means you have to optimize the diminishing amount of heat

Above: When you have a tunnel garden, you may have to open up the ends on sunny days to let the hot air escape from the protected area. Cover again before the sun goes down.

Above right: Old recycled windows and a raised bed make another kind of protected garden.

that reaches them from the winter sun. You can cover individual plants with gallon glass jars, but you'll need many, many jars to do this. An alternative method is to bend a long sheet of fiberglass over the row of plants or seedings. When you close the ends with a board, you'll also keep out sparrows that tear out lettuce seedlings. You can substitute panes of glass fastened together to form a box over a row of plants or seedings.

Old windows, a sheet of clear plastic or anything that lets light through can be placed over the plants. Just keep the material off the leaves to avoid sunburn—or even frost burn at night. If you want to buy such panes together with their special fasteners, look in seed catalogs for *cloches*. This is a French term for covers. But they are expensive compared to recycled covers.

Another device—a result of the plastics revolution—is called Wall o' Water®. It can be bought through catalogs and at some nurseries. It is a large tube made up of a number of little tubes that are filled with water from the top. One device protects one plant. They are tricky to fill and to keep upright, but once erected they will allow light to reach the plant through the water. The water is warmed during the day and releases heat during the night. You'll need a lot of them if you have a large garden.

It's possible to keep the soil warm by laying clear plastic on the ground between the rows of vegetables. Provided the roots are growing—and they need warm soil for this to take place—the tops will also grow, even in cold air. Clear plastic will encourage weed growth; black plastic will prevent it. Contrary to what you might think, black plastic is not as effective as clear plastic to warm the soil.

Tunnel Gardening

The first cold snap of winter reminds us that plants must have warmth if they are to continue growing. The cold is a double-edged sword. It is

This time of year, expect a lot of fruit, particularly pomegranates and citrus, to split. Not much can be done about this except to dispose of the damaged fruit before it attracts insects. The cause? Summer sun hardens the fruit skins. The hard, brittle skin splits as the fruit increases in size.

welcome because deciduous fruit trees need the chilling and a rest from growing if they are to produce the next year. But we also want our winter vegetables to keep growing.

Tunnel gardening, creating a protective covering over your vegetable plants, lets you capture the sun's heat to make a microclimate 20F or 30F warmer than the outside. You change winter into spring and spring into summer. It's an adaptation from commercial vegetable growers who lay clear plastic over their growing plants during winter.

To make a tunnel, you need a framework over the vegetable bed. This is most easily done by using construction mesh, the 6-inch-square material, to make an arch. Share the purchase with a friend to get an economical price. Cut off 10-foot lengths from the 100-foot roll you buy. Rolls comes in widths of 5 or 6 feet.

A 10-foot length makes a nice arch over a 4-foot-wide bed. This can be neatly covered by a 12-foot-wide roll of clear plastic (4 or 6 mils thick). The extra 2 feet width of the plastic enables you to anchor it down on the sides with bricks. Leave extra plastic at the ends so you can close up the tunnel. Add 10 feet to the length of the bed when you buy the plastic. Fold and hold the ends down with more bricks. Four arches of mesh will be enough for a bed 20 feet long.

On sunny days, keep the tunnel closed and allow moisture to build up inside. Moist air absorbs heat and retains it better than dry air. You'll save water, too, because moisture condenses on the inside of the film and drips back to the ground. But check plants frequently to be sure they don't get too hot. Also monitor them for aphids and molds, which can be encouraged by the warm atmosphere. On hot days open up one end—or perhaps both—to ventilate and cool plants. Don't let the soil dry out; check it often, especially during periods of warm weather.

Use tunnels for the next three or four months of cool weather to keep wintertime vegetables growing vigorously. In early March, a tunnel is an ideal place to jump-start summer crops such as corn and squash. Pepper plants and tomato plants can be set out earlier, too, inside a protective tunnel.

Using a Cold Frame

If you are handy with hammer and nails, you can make a *cold frame*. This is basically a glass-covered box in which you grow seedlings and young plants during cooler weather prior to setting them out in the garden after temperatures warm up.

Like tunnel gardening, a cold frame is a sunlight-trapping device, so build it to face south. Make the front wall as low as possible to let in the sunshine. Keep the lid on during cool weather, but slide it off a little when things get hot. If you don't have a sunny place in your yard, there's little point in making a cold frame—unless you want to turn it into a hot bed.

Making a Hot Bed

A hot bed is a cold frame featuring a soil-heating cable. The electric company now provides the heat instead of the sun, but plants still need some sunshine to grow strongly. Old windows make good covers. The walls can be constructed from old boards, bricks or blocks. A hot bed is a temporary structure, so you don't want to get fancy, just functional. Make the front wall 1 foot high and the back wall at least 2 feet high. Slope the side walls, making them airtight with the lid.

If you can't find any old windows, you can make an inexpensive lid from corrugated fiberglass. Start with an 8-foot length and make two 4-foot lengths by cutting across the middle. Place these side by side to give you a 4-foot-square top for your structure. Frame it with 2- by 2-inch redwood. If the walls are wood, you can hinge it at the back. If the walls are brick, you'll have to slide the cover to get ventilation. A loose lid can blow away in the wind, so hinges are preferred.

Spread the soil-heating cable on the ground and cover it with hardware cloth to protect it from sharp tools. An inch or two of soil over the hardware cloth spreads the heat and retains it, but it takes height from the inside of the structure. Some gardeners spread 8 or 9 inches of good soil mix and grow their seedlings directly in it. Tall plants go to the back and seedling trays are placed at the shallow front end.

As with the tunnel, make sure plants and soil don't dry out or get too hot. It's not a hard task, but it's important to keep a regular eye on things.

The First Freeze

Often, the first half of November is mild and pleasant. The weather changes imperceptibly—getting nicer every day. Then one night we get a sharp freeze, which seems to have some connection with the full moon. Be ready for this event, because it's going to be a killing frost. It comes at a time when a lot of summertime vegetables have put on fresh new growth after their summer misery. Even fruit trees and vines may have unwittingly produced vulnerable new growth that will be killed by the cold.

Green Tomatoes

The greatest by-product of the frost will most likely be lots of green tomatoes. Too many, perhaps. You'll have to get out your cookbooks and make relishes, pickles, jams and pies.

Individual fruit can be wrapped in newspaper and set aside to ripen in their own time. An alternative is to pick all the fruit, one by one, and store them in boxes of dry sawdust. Put some fruit in a warmish place for quick results and others in a cool place for later. Some gardeners pull the whole plant out of the ground—roots and all—and hang it in a cool, airy place for the fruit to ripen. In fact, it's a good idea to save some space in a garage or storage shed where you can hang up complete plants. The fruit will gradually ripen on the vine for you.

If we don't get a frosty mid-November surprise, plants will continue to grow unharmed, although their growth will be much slower.

Bush Beans

Bush beans should continue to please. Pick frequently to encourage them to keep producing flowers and pods. Bolster growth with a side dressing of ammonium phosphate using a teaspoon per plant. Incorporate it into the soil carefully so as not to damage the roots, then wash it down with a good irrigation.

Becoming a Weather Expert

That first frost probably surprised you. Nevertheless, you must have been comforted in the knowledge that summertime trees are safe as long as they are not growing. And, being the good gardener that you are, you held back on irrigating and fertilizing a few weeks ago, so your trees didn't suffer.

Cover frost-tender plants before the sun goes down if you think there'll be a frost that night. Take the cover off in the morning to let the sun warm things up again.

November
In Your Garden

The cold temperatures you experience in your garden may be markedly different than those of the official weather reports. To find out where your garden stands, begin to take systematic temperature recordings at the first of the month. If you are determined to help frost-tender plants get through a cold winter, you'll want to know how quickly it's getting cold. You also should know how many degrees warmer or cooler it is at your place than at the official recording station. This will help you decide whether to be complacent or concerned when a frost warning is issued.

Go to a hardware store or a nursery and buy a *minimum-recording thermometer*. It has a little metal bar on the cold side of the gauge that is moved by the column of mercury as the temperature falls. When temperatures rise again, the mercury moves away from the bar and leaves it where it rested. At any comfortable hour of the day, out you go to read last night's recorded low at your place. Mark your coldest temperature on a chart to see how it differs from that at the official recording station and from the predicted low. On a sheet of graph paper (four squares to the inch), make the bottom line the days of the month from November 1 through January 30. On the left side mark the temperature in intervals of 5F, from 0F at the bottom through 90F near the top of the page. Follow the weather reports. Use one color to mark the night's actual low temperature on your chart, another to record the "official" temperature and another to mark tomorrow night's predicted low. You'll soon discover whether temperatures are falling steadily. You'll learn whether you are colder or warmer than the official weather station and if radio and television forecasts are accurate enough to be useful. (See photo, page 131.)

If temperatures fall a few degrees each night in a regular pattern, your plants will harden off nicely and will be able to withstand the freeze when it comes. If the forecasts prove to be accurate, you can rely on them in the future and protect your plants only when you need to. If temperatures at your place are consistently warmer than those at the official recording station, even by a few degrees, you don't have to worry so much when they say it's going to freeze.

Hang your minimum-recording thermometer near plants you are concerned about surviving the cold. Don't hang it inside a citrus tree, where it will be protected, or against a wall, where it will be warmed by residual heat. If you have frost-tender plants scattered around your landscape, you may need more than one thermometer. You'll be surprised how temperatures vary between an open southern exposure and a walled-in northern patio.

Dispose of Ashes

The first cold snap, if it is a sharp one, sets people to lighting fires in their houses. It's a nice Thanksgiving gesture to friends and a comfort to themselves. Not as comforting are the ashes. What to do with them?

People from eastern states remember putting fireplace ashes on their gardens. Ashes supply potash, a plant food, and make an acid soil sweeter. Our desert soils usually contain sufficient potash and they are already too alkaline. Putting ashes on a garden makes things worse—

not better. The same is true for the compost pile. Send the ashes to the dump, even if it seems wasteful.

Fun with Sweet Potatoes

If you have an uncooked sweet potato or two left over from the holiday feast—and don't particularly want to eat another for a long time—you can give the children an interesting indoor-gardening assignment.

Help them slice the root lengthwise. Dust the flesh with sulphur to prevent decay. Place the two halves, flat side down, in a shallow pan with drainage holes containing a sandy soil mix or plain, coarse sand. The sand should be 3 inches deep to allow for the extensive root growth to come. Put the dish in a sunny window and keep the sand moist. Sweet potatoes are warm-weather plants. Some people grow the potato in a pan of plain water, but you must change the water often to keep it sweet.

After a month or two trim back the new shoots or train them up on a framework. The old root shrinks as its food reserves are used up by new growth. Now's the time to add houseplant food to the water—the usual tablespoon in a gallon. Luxuriant leaf growth calls for a lot of nitrogen. You'll have to supply it because there's none in the sand or water. Fertilize and water—and there's your own sweet-potato bed.

If your children are imaginative, they can train the more vigorous shoots up strings attached to the ceiling. Of course, they can't move the dish now, so they should have selected its permanent place in their room. Train the vines up the strings then guide them along horizontally placed strings to the corner of the room. When the vines reach the corner, guide them into a left turn and then another, and another until they come back from where they started. Your children will have a room of greenery and an enjoyable sense of achievement.

Next April, take slips off the room plant and put them in pots of sandy potting soil. In May or June when the soil is well warmed and when the slips have a bunch of strong roots on them, set them out in well-prepared soil.

In years past you may have yearned for one of these and been disappointed when you discovered that local nurseries didn't have any plants in early summer when you needed them. Remember that we have short seasons in the desert, so you must plan ahead and start early. You can't get seeds and the plant doesn't make any, so get an early start with a sweet-potato plant in your warm house.

November
In Your Garden

December

December's weather is unreliable. It may be rainy or it may be dry and sunny. The only thing that's certain is that the days are short. For most of the month the sun rises soon after 7 a.m. and sets before 5:30 p.m. This doesn't give you time to do anything in the yard before or after work; only the weekends are left. Fortunately, there's not a lot to do. Short days and low temperatures mean plants aren't very active either.

Use December as a study month for gardens yet to come. There are vegetable seeds to choose and fruit trees to consider. If you are going to plant bare-root trees, which are less expensive than container-grown trees, you must have everything ready for the rush that inevitably occurs.

Some years it snows in December. Snow itself isn't all that cold, and as it melts it provides a natural drip irrigation that soaks the soil. Snow is unwelcome only because it is heavy when it falls in quantity and can break branches of junipers and other leafy evergreens. Brush snow off your plants to save them from damage.

There's not a lot of urgent work to be done in the December landscape, aside from repairing any damage caused by storms. Plan your springtime plantings, clean and sharpen tools, overhaul engines or clean out the garden shed, if you must. Then go in and sit by the fire (don't spread the ashes in the garden), dream over the garden catalogs, and read a good landscaping book.

This saguaro is short of water, as shown by the compressed pleats of its trunk. In summer this might indicate the need for a good watering but during winter the desert's cacti can withstand a freeze if they are not growing and have a high concentration of nutrients in their systems.

🌱 Featured Plants for December

Saguaro Cactus

It's common to see a bird's nest built in the crook of a saguaro arm, where it branches from the main trunk. The nests soak up the water that runs down the plant's flutes. In years when the desert enjoys prolonged winter rains, this can cause problems for saguaros. The soggy nests encourage rots and weaken the arms, which can be quite heavy. With time, the arms can be damaged to the extent they fall from the main trunk. During periods of steady winter rains, it's wise to preserve the saguaro's health and remove the nests, even if it seems as if it's an unkind thing to do.

↓ Soil Preparation

Composting

Leaves are a common commodity in December and are ideal materials for composting. Some years we get a sharp frost that knocks them all off at once. That's good for people who aren't too keen on sweeping up because it's once and for all, and they can handle that. But if it happens that way, your bin is filled to overflowing. This often occurs in mid-December.

Fallen leaves are better than money in the bank for home gardeners. They will make a beautiful soil additive when the time comes to dig a flower bed or plant a tree. All you have to do is rake them into a pile and surround that pile with stout wire so that they don't blow away. Keep the pile lightly moist, turn it when its temperature reaches 160F, and beneficial bacteria will do the rest. They will decompose your unwanted leaves as well as any additional kitchen vegetable scraps, weeds and garden clippings into a suitable alternative to expensive peat moss or "forest mulch." With proper turnings—three or four of them—you'll have good, ready-to-use compost in three or four months.

Be ready for this leaf fall. Compost is best made in a frame above ground, even though a lot of books mention compost pits. A heavy wire frame works well. Some people try to make it in plastic bags and garbage bins. If you want good, quickly made compost, you must allow air to reach the bacteria that break down the vegetative matter. No air means undesirable bacteria get to work. They make a smelly, soggy mess instead of a light, crumbly leaf mold.

Keep the heap of collected leaves moist with an occasional sprinkle. They will heat up in a day or two from bacterial activity. Temperatures of 120F are easily reached. These will kill weed seeds and some disease organisms. Use your soil probe to gauge the heat. If it remains cold, there is no bacterial activity. The bacteria may need moisture, which you will have to supply by watering the pile if rainfall is scant. Or the bacteria may be too wet and short of air so the pile needs to be turned. If you want compost in a hurry, simply turn the pile to provide oxygen for the bacteria. Turn once a week, keep the pile moist and you will have usable material in about six weeks.

You can add in any vegetative material from the kitchen, but don't use your compost pile as a garbage heap. Meat scraps invite vermin, tin cans and plastic don't decay and glass bottles are a danger.

Some gardeners value homemade compost so much that they buy bags of leaves from neighborhood children who have raked them up from other people's yards. Buy leaves—and help a child through Christmas. In turn, you'll help your garden produce more next summer. Plenty of organic matter in the soil keeps it moist longer, and that saves on your water bill.

☘ Planting

Seldom is it worth the effort to set out plants or sow seeds this time of year. It's too cold in spite of the sunshine—even when compared to the rest of the country that is under snow and sleet. Gardening has slowed considerably, and whatever is growing is growing slowly. Active people want to be doing something—and therein lies a danger. If you cannot contain your energy, go and dig some planting holes. They should be 5 feet square and 5 feet deep, so plan before you start digging. (See photo, page 122.)

Planting in Bags

One way to make the most of the waning December sun is to plant directly into a bag of soil amendment such as peat moss or potting soil mix. You don't even have to open the bag. Don't use steer manure because it's too strong. For more information, see page 17.

Plants can also be set out in your compost pile. This can be either the new one that is steaming away with fresh leaves, or the old one that has been livened up with a layer of fresh leaves. Your plants benefit from the heat and the decomposing organic matter will provide it.

Lettuce

A few years ago, the newspapers reported that something had gone wrong with commercial lettuce plantings in southern California. A number of gardeners took a gamble and sowed lettuce seeds in December. They germinated well and grew nicely to reach harvest size just as supermarket prices rose to double than normal. It's rare that you succeed at playing the futures market in your home garden, but lettuce does its best in winter.

Usually the first seed is sown during September and thereafter at monthly intervals. Following this schedule, the first harvest is ready mid-October. The succession of sowings gives you a continuous supply until May. It's a highly useful and productive crop for the colder months of the year.

Although lettuce prefers cooler temperatures, we get a little impatient with its slower growth during the month of December. We can overcome this to some extent by using ammonium nitrate in place of the usual ammonium sulphate. Use a little less because it is stronger: 33 percent nitrogen compared to 21 percent nitrogen for an equal amount of ammonium sulphate. Pale plants will green up within a week and their size will increase, too. A light application, such as a teaspoon shared between three or four plants every two weeks, will push your crop along.

Head lettuce does not grow nearly as well as leaf types. And there are many leaf varieties from which to choose. Change from one variety of leaf lettuce to another as you make successive sowing, and you can look forward to an interesting variety of salads.

Head lettuce varieties take 75 days—or more—to mature, whereas leaf types need only 40 days or so. We are back at the principle of desert gardening: You have a number of short seasons at your disposal. In any event, it's best to grow quick-maturing varieties.

Birds go for lettuce seedlings in a big way. Protect the rows with a covering of chicken wire. You shouldn't have trouble from harvester ants, which are typically dormant in December, but there may be cutworms in the soil. Consider purchasing lettuce seedlings from a nursery to maintain your interval plantings if birds and cutworms get the better of you.

Fruit Trees

A number of new varieties of fruit trees requiring a minimum amount of winter chilling are becoming available. Visit your favorite nursery and ask to see their order catalogs. Read the descriptions of fruit-tree varieties. Talk with someone knowledgeable, then place an order. Dig the planting holes to keep you out of gardening mischief. Postpone pruning in December and pass on the fertilizing as well. There is less watering to do. Be ready to take action come the new year.

Plant fruit trees where they can be enjoyed during all seasons. For example, locate them where you can see the blossoms. Perhaps use them to screen out something unsightly. But don't let them hide a pleasant view. In other words—think. Don't act on an impulse. In December you have time to think.

◖ Watering

Part of the "so little to do at this time of year" syndrome is that there isn't a great need to irrigate. Normal winter rains are gentle and long lasting. Even if they don't materialize, our plants seem to get by comfortably because the lower temperatures are not so low they stop growth altogether.

Winter rains soak into the ground because they are gentle. In some years the soil is well watered with the purest of water—and deep down. If you have been having salt problems, perhaps caused by overfertilizing or salty water, or by stingy irrigating in summer when the water rates were high, now is your chance to treat them.

A deep irrigation will leach those salts down past the root zone, even if the plants don't need the moisture. A deep watering will do far more good in wet soil than it will trying to get through dry soil first. Furthermore, the salts are already in solution from the rains, meaning they are more easily carried through the soil and away from the root zone.

If winter rains are continuous, the weather is usually warm and vegetables that were set out in October continue to grow nicely. You'll be rewarded with a good harvest.

Don't irrigate with ice-cold water. This is especially true of container plants. They live in a warmer soil because they are usually in a sheltered part of the patio or porch. Be especially careful with houseplants. Keep your watering container full of water in the room where the plants are located.

Keep the wildflowers growing. If it doesn't rain much in December, water them occasionally. Once a week might be too often, but they are shallow rooted and need some attention. During one of these waterings give the plants some ammonium nitrate if their color is a little pale. Scatter it on wet soil at the rate of 1 pound to 100 square feet and water it in well. Be sure to wash the fertilizer off the leaves. Nourish wildflowers as they grow for the most profuse blooms in March and April.

◝ Fertilizing

Don't fertilize any plants going into dormancy. There's a temptation—especially if December is mild—to notice new, tender growth and think it needs a push. The truth is quite the contrary; some plants arc better off if they stop growing. Deciduous fruit trees and vines need a rest—and a long one, if possible. Citrus trees need to be hardened off against forthcoming freezes. Remember, you fertilize plants that are growing or are about to grow. If your fruit trees are entering dormancy, don't keep them growing by applying fertilizer. Rather, slow their growth by withholding an irrigation. But don't overdo it. Plant roots must receive regular moisture to survive.

Vegetable Plants

Keep your vegetable plants growing by fertilizing with frequent but small applications of ammonium nitrate—a teaspoon for two or three plants every two weeks. Always apply dry fertilizer to wet soil—preferably halfway through an irrigation. If you scatter dry fertilizer on top of plant leaves instead of carefully putting it on the ground, wash off any crystals that rest on the foliage. A single teaspoon of ammonium nitrate dissolves very quickly and completely in one gallon of water. Pour this solution on moist soil around the root zone of your actively growing winter vegetables.

✷ Pruning

December is almost pruning time but not quite; wait for complete dormancy. The best time is when the sap is down, which will be sometime in January or February. Some people are impatient, and some love the sound of chain saws. This often leads to imprudent pruning. Don't rush the job. In the case of deciduous trees, wait until the leaves are off the tree. Next, take a test snipping of a twig or two. If sap runs out the end, the tree is not completely dormant and it's not yet time to prune. In the case of palm trees, don't cut off any green fronds. In the case of tall trees of any kind, don't saw off the branches all at the same height. In other words, don't *top* your trees.

What happens if you prune too soon? The sugary sap that comes out the ends of the cut branches acts like glue. Any fungus and bacteria spores blowing in the wind gets caught in it. The sap provides food for the spores, and the spores grow into the space between the bark and the wood. Your tree is now infected with either sooty canker (a fungus) or slime flux (a bacteria). Either will kill your tree. When you prune, use a spray can of pruning paint to protect the cut ends from these invaders.

You can see mistletoe growing in desert trees after they have dropped their leaves. It breaks off easily, but comes back after a while. To stop regeneration, tie black plastic around the branch and tie it in place at the ends. When the mistletoe grows again it's in the dark and it won't survive.

✒ Pests and Problems

Take Advantage of Winter Bareness

In December, the leaves (or most of them) have fallen from deciduous trees and shrubs, and you can notice many things that you could not see when plants were in full foliage. Walk around your landscape trees and remove twisted, damaged branches, or branches that cross one another. Remove branches that are inflicting damage to buildings or other structures. Ornamental trees may need to be thinned so that the wind blows through the canopy, rather than catching it, toppling the tree. (A particular hazard with young mesquites.) Don't top the tree—it will only cause it to produce an overgrowth of branches and leaves.

Mistletoe is easy to see when branches are bare. It is a parasite and should be removed. Don't cut off an entire branch affected by mistletoe if you can avoid it. Severe pruning will cause your tree to lose its natural appearance, much like topping. Instead, pull the mistletoe off—it's loosely attached—and gather and dispose of the berry-laden branches. Leave mistletoe on the ground and birds will eat the berries, spreading the seeds. If the mistletoe resprouts in the spring, pull it off again. Mistletoe that comes back again and again can be killed by wrapping it with black plastic, tying at the ends. (See photo, opposite.)

Prune landscape trees lightly to preserve their natural appearance. Deciduous fruit trees should be severely cut back in January.

Protecting Citrus Fruit from Birds

Fairly large, neat holes appear in fruit and there are clusters of little brown gnats at the entrances. The holes were put there by thirsty woodpeckers who have learned that there is sweet, tasty food inside

Frequent winter rains encourage snails to come out of the ground and to wander over our gardens, eating young seedlings. They'll readily go into a can that contains a small amount of beer. When the can is full of snails, throw it in the dumpster.

those brightly colored balls that hang on certain trees in our yards. Cover the tree with a white sheet.

Remove any damaged oranges and grapefruit from the tree because more gnats will be attracted by the juice smell.

It is said that birds can be kept away from ripening fruit if you spray the whole tree with a solution containing Sloanes Liniment®. Add 2 tablespoons of liniment and a dash of detergent to emulsify the mixture to 1 gallon of warm water. This spray protects pyracantha berries from birds. If you are doubtful of its value on citrus, spray a branch or two and hope that its odor will envelop the whole tree. Otherwise, you might be deterred from eating the fruit yourself!

Snails

A night of gentle rain can bring them out in dozens. On a cloudy morning you catch them far from their hiding places. Step on them and crunch them, or buy them from your children at ten for a penny. You can increase the rate to a cent apiece when the children get bored with their collecting. It's easy money anyway, and it stays in the family.

But where do snails come from in the first place? When you buy container plants grown in coastal California, look in the soil. That's how snails are usually introduced. Don't bring them into your garden if you can prevent it. If you see any, pick them off and crunch them.

To reduce snail populations, keep the soil surface as dry as possible by irrigating less frequently and in the morning so the sun dries everything out. Remove excess shade created by low branches of trees and shrubs. Snails are a part of the natural chain of destruction, but will, unfortunately, eat young seedlings when they are tired of consuming decaying vegetation.

Snails can be enticed by beer and become trapped or drowned in it. Lay a beer can with a little beer still in it on the ground so the opening is at ground level The snails go in—but don't come out. (See photo page 149.) Put the can of snails in the trash for a journey to the dump.

If you are not a beer person or prefer to drink your beer until the can is empty, snail baits are available at nurseries. A lot of gardeners don't like them because they look like cat food or breakfast cereal. You are supposed to sprinkle them around your garden for the snails to bump into. Although they may have a component attractive to snails, many people think the poisonous pellets can be dangerous to children, birds and pets.

Pests on Winter Vegetables

If you have winter vegetables such as broccoli, cabbage, cauliflower and lettuce, there might be something nasty lurking on them. Take a close look in the heart of the plants and on the back of the leaves. That's where grey aphids hide when they first attack plants. The early appearance is one of a puckered leaf with a pale blotch on it. Aphids are on the other side sucking away the juices. Grey aphids look like a speck of wood ash lying in a cupped portion of the leaf. That's their way of hiding. A spotty pale color and crinkling of the leaves will tell you something is wrong. Later on, the wilting plants show complete stress and the aphids are obvious by their masses. An infestation happens quickly.

Take a close look on the midrib of each leaf. That's where the slender-bodied looper caterpillars line themselves up. Because they have just eaten your plant's leaves, they are an identical green color and hard to see. Take your time. Remove these pests as you find them. Don't wait for tomorrow because they will be twice as destructive. Rub them out using a finger and thumb. Or spray them with soapy water or a 50-50 solution of rubbing alcohol and water if the plants are close to harvest. If the plants are young, spray with diazinon or Malathion 50®. These chemicals have a residual life of about 10 days, but read and follow the label before applying to determine their safe use.

✓ Special Considerations

Cold Protection

To keep your plants growing during cold weather, erect a construction-mesh arch and cover it with clear plastic. Tuck in the ends to make everything airtight. Moist air trapped inside heats up nicely. During hot days you will have to open the ends to ventilate your temporary greenhouse.

If a freeze is in the forecast, cover the structure with a light blanket as the sun goes down. This retains heat accumulated during the day. Remove the blanket in the morning after the sun shines on the bed.

Have frost protection materials handy; cold weather is unpredictable and you may need to protect plants in a hurry. Be prepared with light blankets or heavy sheets, extension cords and low-wattage light bulbs. Frost warnings often come at the last minute—or it seems that we react to them at the last minute. You don't want to be looking all over the place at night for items that you need immediately.

Prickly pears can be weakened by a freeze. If so, the frozen pads tend to snap off and fall to the ground. This may not bother you because this is how prickly pears grow naturally into thickets. The fallen pads easily root where they rest on the soil. If you are a tidy

Prickly pear plants fall apart after a freeze. It's Mother Nature's way of pruning and propagating. The pads easily root where they fall and, in this case, a thicket will develop where pack rats and other animals can hide. It's better to clean up and use the pads as planting material in another place.

Above: Solid walls around a landscape tend to retain pockets of cold air, reducing temperatures around plants.

Above right: Even small drainage holes such as these in the wall allow the cold air to drain away from plants, increasing temperatures.

landscaper, however, you may want to clean up after a freeze. You can discard the fallen branches or you can cleanly remove pads and plant them where you want plants to grow. If you plant the pads right away, dust the ends with powdered sulphur to ward off fungus and bacteria. Otherwise, store the pieces in a sheltered carport or under a tree where they won't be further damaged by more frosty nights. The cut ends will scab over on their own and will be ready for planting in two or three weeks, even two or three months. Plant the pieces on a mound for good drainage; succulents easily rot in cold, wet soil.

Containers and Cold Temperatures

Move containers into sunny, sheltered places where they will gather daytime heat that will carry plants through the night. If the nights turn frosty, cover with a sheet or light blanket.

Winter Vegetables

Winter vegetables set out in mid-October will grow well during December, but growth is slow and a little disappointing. If you don't want to go to the trouble of making a tunnel they can be helped along by placing a gallon glass jug over each one. This creates an individual greenhouse for each plant, keeping them warm and protected from cold winds. A glass jar pushed into the soil also keep cutworms from the plant.

Preparing Citrus for a Freeze

Don't let frost warnings frighten you into picking citrus fruit. It's true that fruit will be damaged if it is exposed to three hours of temperatures at 28F or below, but the weather forecast won't tell you how long the coldest predicted temperature will last. Cover your tree and provide heat inside it, but don't pick the fruit to avoid possible damage unless the forecast is for several days of continuous freezing temperatures. If you have lots of trees and few blankets, first protect the limes, then the lemons, then the oranges, then the tangerines (you're probably eating them by now, anyway), and finally the grapefruits, which are more hardy than the others. If you feel you must pick, begin with the exposed outer fruit. Fruit inside the canopy are somewhat protected by the foliage. Citrus fruit is better stored on the tree, all things being equal.

The color change in citrus fruit serves as a reminder to get our frost-protection materials handy. It's hard to believe that such beautiful sunny days can go hand in hand with freezing nights—but they do. And a freeze often comes quickly. Be prepared.

As mentioned on page 151, have a number of light blankets or heavy sheets ready. Secondhand stores are good places to find them if you have none that you're ready to sacrifice. For each tree hang a portable light fixture or two and cover with a bucket to protect the light bulb from moisture.

Watch your thermometer and compare your temperatures with those at the airport and the forecasts. Be aware of what's going on by keeping a gardener's diary, as suggested on page 156. Be ready at short notice to cover your trees and set out the light bulbs. Keep a flashlight handy as well in case you have to work at night.

Don't rely on irrigating to protect your trees from freezing. You'd have to flood the whole yard 6 inches deep to achieve your purpose, perhaps every night.

Ordering from Seed Catalogs

Seed catalogs begin to arrive in late December. The seed companies are at last realizing that desert gardening regions have a different time frame compared to that in eastern states. Even so, you'll still see invitations to get the free bonus offer if you order before May 15! Here in

Below left: A plastic tunnel keeps the moisture in and reduces your need to water, since it condenses on the plastic and drops back onto the soil. Also see photo page 138.

Below: Another way to conserve moisture is to sow seeds in trenches and cover with clear plastic.

the desert we've usually got everything planted by that date. We order tomato seeds in December and sow them indoors in mid-January.

Catalogs have always been a beautiful stimulant. As we sit by the fire, we are so encouraged by their colorful pictures that we forget the difficulties of gardening in the desert. We plan our "next time around" with enthusiasm and optimism. There's never a negative word in a seed catalog.

Don't go overboard with new varieties, although some may be better than the old ones. And it's nice to know plant breeders are working on types suitable for home gardens. They have not been fully tested under desert conditions. Until recently we had to take leftovers from commercial field varieties that were developed for one-time harvesting. Expensive machinery obliged the farmer to gather as much as he could in one pass. He didn't want to pick a second or third time. He likes *determinate* plants, those that grow to a certain size and then stop. A home gardener, on the other hand, likes to pick a little something for several weeks from *indeterminate* plants. They continue to grow without a size limit until freezing temperatures take care of them. Look for these terms as you read a seed catalog.

Although the catalogs are wooing home gardeners, their target audiences are the population centers—the old cities, not the new ones. Most of these populated regions are in the Midwest and East. This means desert gardeners have to be particularly perceptive in ordering their seeds. Many of the All-American winners are not suitable for desert gardening. As an example, a few years ago new sweet-pepper varieties were praised because they displayed their fruit well above the foliage. A picture showed a gardener gazing admiringly at his colorful fruits. Here in the desert, any fruit that shows off in this manner gets badly sunburned and is quickly rendered useless. We need vegetables that keep their fruit tucked well under the foliage.

Ignore superlatives like "jumbo," "giant" and "colossal." By their nature, these are slow growers. Don't be influenced by statements like "the biggest fruit we've ever seen" or "the sweetest and juiciest."

A lot of popular varieties originate from European countries. Their seeds do well in the Midwest, where growing seasons are long. Many don't do as well in the desert where seasons are short. Surprisingly—at least at first—varieties from Canada do well in the desert. But on second thought, Canadians have short growing seasons, too—occasioned by cold and snow, whereas ours are caused by heat. An ideal plant produces early and maintains production through thick and thin, or, in other words, in spite of weather changes.

Seed companies can't tell you about this. They haven't carried out a trial planting in your backyard. Neither do you have the resources nor the time, but your nearby land-grant college could be doing it for you. Ask your extension service agent for information about local seed variety trials.

When selecting plants, consider more than total yield. Instead, choose a variety that will give early and sustained production throughout the summer months. There's little point in having no yield most of the year, then a great heap of tomatoes all in one week. It's the same with beans, melons and squash—or any vegetable that produces fruit. Of course, you want good flavor, but catalogs cannot tell you this. Flavor is a personal thing. You must experience it yourself.

Recently, catalogs have begun to use a number in parentheses after the variety name. This tells you how many days after planting out or sowing seed it will be until the first harvest. Don't ignore it, because it's a useful piece of information. Count the days of the variety you think you would like to plant, and of the season available to you. Match them up. For example, if there are less than 100 days of good growing weather—neither too hot nor too cold—it is obviously risky to try a variety that needs more than 100 days to produce its first fruit. Production should continue, of course, long after that first glorious day.

Growing Flowers From Seed

Seed catalogs also inspire and tempt us to try new kinds of flowers. Producing your own flowering plants, is, however, more complex than growing your own vegetable plants. It's trickier because flower seeds are often small, take a long time to grow to flowering stage and require more careful management to mature. Most towns have nurseries that will provide us with a wide range of suitable plants at the right time of year. The prices are reasonable and you can often see the flower colors before you buy. You can even add that color to your landscape the very day you buy plants.

Sowing seed in the ground means watching for weeds germinating the same time, while also protecting plants from birds, rabbits, caterpillars, grasshoppers and harvester ants. It means patiently waiting several weeks before plants reach flowering stage. If you insist on growing your own, use 4-inch containers filled with a growing medium composed of equal parts sand, perlite, vermiculite and peat moss. (All these ingredients are available at nurseries.) After sowing seed, place containers in a sheltered spot where they will be exposed to several hours of sunshine. Keep the planting mixture moist. Be patient, and within about 10 weeks, the seedlings will be large enough to set out into the garden.

Fall Color

Some years we get to enjoy fall colors in November; some years we have to wait until December. Find out the names of those colorful plants that please you and consider including them in your landscape next spring. Trees that thrill us with autumn color include locust, chinaberry, poplar, cottonwood, pistache and ash. Peach, apricot and pomegranate trees are colorful, too. A persimmon tree, with its orange fruit hanging at the tips of bare winter branches, makes a wonderful living Christmas ornament in your landscape; be sure to plant it where you'll see it. Another "Christmassy" plant is the shrub *Photinia fraseri;* its bright new red leaves sit atop a green shrub like glowing candles. The pads of Santa Rita prickly pear turn purplish as the cold weather continues. Other colorful plants include the small wild poinsettia (it seeds itself far and wide), purple fountain grass, New Zealand flax,

December
In Your Garden

_____

_____

_____

_____

_____

_____

nandina and hopseed bush. All have leaves that turn dark brown or purple in cold weather.

Your Own Gardening Diary

Reputable seed catalogs are useful guides. So is a garden diary. You can read back and discover what did well for you. You can avoid repeating a mistake. If you haven't kept a diary, this is an excellent month to get organized. Make a New Year's resolution, and begin recording your gardening thoughts and experiences. Consider using the "In Your Garden" notation columns provided in this book. (See at right.)

Christmas Gifts for Gardeners

Early this month, start thinking about Christmas gifts for your gardening friends. You may have to order certain items from mail-order companies or companies on the Internet. First, know the level of your friend's interest or competence. It would be a mistake to challenge him or her too much by giving a plant or seeds that won't grow well in the desert. This is particularly true with children who are just showing an interest in gardening. Don't smother that enthusiasm by starting them on difficult projects that will probably fail.

A sprout kit is a good gift for a child. It can be homemade, or fancy ones are available from stores. Glass mason jars with wire-mesh lids let you drain the water. A selection of seeds, such as alfalfa, mung beans, cabbage and radish, can be found at health food stores. Don't buy packets of seeds for sprouting from the nursery. They are often coated with poisonous chemicals to protect them from soil diseases.

What could be nicer—for the receiver, at least—than a "Certificate of Promise?" A promise to dig a planting hole measuring 5 feet by 5 feet and 5 feet deep. And to fill it up again after planting!

Fruit trees make wonderful gifts. They are available at nurseries in containers. These will survive being left on a doorstep overnight. The problem of wrapping such a gift can be overcome by using a gift certificate that allows the recipient to choose the tree.

A friend living in a townhouse is sure to appreciate a half whiskey barrel, especially if it has been sanded, oiled and drainage holes drilled in preparation for planting. Bags of potting soil are not very exciting, but they are useful and welcome. A bottle of insecticide might offend, but a quality pump-up sprayer is another story.

It's nice to own good-quality tools, but we often buy the bargains for ourselves. Buy your friend a good set of hand tools that will last a lifetime. He is sure to take care of them. And you've turned him into a better gardener without his knowing it. Good tools are a pleasure to own and a joy to use.

A minimum-recording thermometer that records "how cold it got last night" will be appreciated by weather-aware gardeners, as will a rain gauge by the optimist. A soil-heating cable is a good gift for the gardener who likes to grow his own seedlings. And then there's the subscription to a gardening magazine, or better yet, a good book on desert gardening!

Index

16–17, 44–45, 92, 147–48

figs, 21, 23, 88, 98

flies, 52. *See also* whiteflies

flowers, 50, 55, 110, 155

foliar feeding, 29–30

freezes, frost, 2, 11, 35, 121, 140; damage from, 19, 31–32, 141; protection from, 151–53

fruit, 24, 56, 85, **139**; and birds, 61–63, 65–66; harvesting, 36–37, 88–89; protection of, 28, 116–17, 130; thinning, 39–40; watering and, 94–95

fungi, 6, 9, 66, 84–85, 87–88, 97, 135

G

galls: bacterial, 31, 33

gardens: cool season, 107–12, 123; preparation of, **13**, 14–15; protected, 137–**38**; tunnel, **134**, **138**–40, **153**; vegetable, 16–18

garlic, 51

geraniums, 23, 64, 93, 113

gophers, 24, 128–30

grapefruit, 11, 23, **24**, 37, 56, 64, 132,152

grapes, 29, 31, **37**, 38–39, 65–66, 74, 84, 88, 96, **98**, 105, 112, 118, 135; cuttings from, 21, 22, 23; pests on, 32, 56, **58**, **59**–60, 81; protecting, 62–63, 85; pruning, **9**–10

grasshoppers, 115, 128

greenhouses, **26**, 27, 131

grey water, 80

grubs, 14, 48, 66, 82, **83**, 99, 113, 115–16

gumming, 46

H

heat stress, 74, 75, 85, 94, 99

hedges, 30–31, 61, 71–72, **81**, 97–98, 127

herbs, 103–4

hornworms, tomato, 57

hot beds, 140

I

insecticidal soap, 27, 32

insecticides, 24, 27, 32, 33, 56, 57–58, 60, 82, 83, 99, 100, 102, 115–16, 126, 127, 128, 151

insects, 14, 19, 32, 46, 52, 71, 81–84, 89, 90, 113–15, 127–28, 150–51; beneficial, 33–34, 73–74; summer, 56–60, 72–73

insect traps, 98

irises, 93, 103

irrigation, 8, 18, **28**, 40, 43, **64**, 79, 80, 147; fertilization and, 19, 135–36; with swimming pool water, 95–96

K

katydids, **128**

L

lacewings, 33

ladybugs, 33–34

lawns, 49, **64**, **65**, **68**, 71, 79, 93, 105–6, 123, 132, 133; irrigating, 80, 95

leaf curl, 57

leafhoppers, 32, 33, 56–57, 72–73, 81

leaf litter, 32

lemons, 23, 37, 56, 90, 132, 152

lettuce, 6, 16, 20, 42, 50, 105, 108, 111, 118, 126, 146

limes, 23, 132, 152

M

Malathion®, 24, 32, 56, 57, 60, 83, 98, 99, 100, 115, 127, 151

manure, 14, 50, 84, 107, 110

melons, 18, 67, 74, 89

mesquite, 24, **36**, 46

mildew, 32-33, 39, 47, 60, 61

mineral oil, 58

Miracle-Gro®, 23, 92

misting, 23

mistletoe, 20, **21**, **148**, 149

mites, 33, 99

moths, 48, **58**, 59

mulberries, **25**, 36, 42, 81

mulch, 44, 51, 70–71, **95**

mushrooms, 87-88, **106**, 118–19

mustard, 10–11

N

nematodes, 66, 99–100

nitrates, 16–17

nitrogen, 7, 30, 12, **106**

nopalitos, 38, 51

nurseries, 26, 122–23

nutgrass, 14, 16, 66

O

okra, 50, 67, 74

oleanders, 21, 23, **31**, 32, 33, **47**, 56, 81, 113

olives, 25, **38**, 39

Olive-Stop®, 25, 39

onions, **12**, 13, 50, 51, 112

oranges, 23, 36–37, 90, 116, 130, 132, 137, **139**, 152

organic matter, 13, 14

P

paint, pruning, 9, 19, 46, 71, 86

palms, 64, **76**, 77, 86, 97, 113

palo verdes, 32, 81, 99

peaches, 23, 24, 29, 55, 74, 81, 84, 88, 98

peas, 103, 134; black-eyed, 50, 67, 74, 77, 118; garden, 18, 105, 109; sweet, 110–**111**

pecans, 29, 40–41, 73, 91–92, 120–21, 132–33

peppers, 26, 43, 46, 104, 112, 119, 154; bell, 27, 64, 74, 118

persimmon, 156

Photinia fraseri, 156

pill bugs, 32, 71

pines, 68, 99–100, 121

planting, 9, 67, 121; in bags, 145–46; fall and winter gardens, 107–12; soil temperature and, 25–26, 42; vegetables, 27, 42, 54–55, 77–78, 134–35

planting beds, **13,** 14–15, 16

planting holes, 2–3

plant ties, **20**, 35, 44, 49, **55**, 65–66

plastic, 16, 17–18, 22–23, 49, 145, **153**; and soil sterilization, **66**–67, 77

poinsettias, 106–7

pollination, 24, 45, 46; corn, 58–59, 102; squash, 52–53, 67; tomato, 51–52

pomegranates, 73, 84, 95, 117, 137, 139

praying mantises, 34, **128**

preemergents, 34–35, 85

prickly pear, 55, 67, 103, 127, **151**, 156; new pads on, 37–38, 51

privet, 23, 32, 56, 88, 113

pruning, 2, 30, **33**, 37, 46, 56, 81, 87, 97–98, 113, 127, 136, 148, 149; frost-damaged plants, 19,31–32; grapes, **9**–10; roses, 40, 106; trees, **7–8**

pyracantha, 21, 22, 150

R

rabbits, 130

radishes, 111, 116, 118, 126

rainfall, 24, 28, 29, 78, 79, 81, 82, 87–88, 90, **91**, 112, 126, 130–31, 146, 147, 150; harvesting, 85–86

roots, 4, 5, 21, 22, 27, 28, 79, 94

RooTone® powder, 22, 92

root stock, 5

root suckers, 36

roses, 21, 23, 32, 36, 40, 51, 92, 106

rosewood, Arizona, 113

rot: fruit and blossom end, 74–75; saguaro, 47, 76

ryegrass, 6, 29, 105, 132, 133

S

saguaro, 47, 50, 55, 76-77, **144**

salts, 29–30, 95–96, 147

sap flow, 7, 46

seed catalogs, 153–55

seeding, 34

seedlings, 109, 110

shade, 65, 74, 85, 88, 90, **94**

shrubs, 6, 69, 132

skeletonizers: grape-leaf, 14, **58**, **59**, 81, 99, 113

slime flux, 9

Sloanes Liniment, 150

snails, 32, **149**, 150

snow, 11, 144

soil, 21–22, 76; preparation of, 3–4, 14–15, 50, 55, 90, **102**, 107, 118–19, 144–45; sterilization of, **66**–67, 77, 100

soil amendment, 17

soil-heating cables, 22

soil probe, **69**, 78–79

soil temperature, 25–26, 42, 123, 131

sooty canker, 9

spinach, 6, 49, 54

sprayers, **29**, 30

squash, 18, 27, 37, 41–42, 50, 54, 74, 77, 90; borers on, 47–48; pollination of, 52–53, 67

squirrels, 24, 63

staking, 20, 35

starter solutions, 43

storm damage, 86

strawberries, 30, 32, 40, 104–5, **125**

succulents, **44**

sulphur, 50, 84, 107, 152; wettable, 32–33, 39, 60, 61

summer blight, 99

summer fallowing, 66

summer stress, 99

sunburn, 88

sweet potato, 23, 75, 143

swimming pool, 95–96

T

tangerines 23, 132, 152

temperatures, 63, 64-65, 74, 142; and winter vegetables, 137–40

terminal buds, 22

termites, 113–14

Texas root rot, 3, 84–85, 99

thermometers: minimum-recording, 142, 156

thinning, 39–40, **134**–35

thrips, 19, 24, 33, 46

Thuricide®, 58

tomatoes, 18, 23, 25, 42–43, 46, 49, 74, 75, 77–78, 84, **87**, 92, 104, 108, 111, 112, 118, 119, 141, 154; pests on, 26–27, 57, 72–73; pollination of, 51–52; shade for, 64–65

transplanting, 121–22

trees, 6, **45**, 68, **69**, 72, 87, 110, 127, 132; fall color and, 155–56; fruit, 3–5, 12, 24–25, **28**, 39–40, 56, 112, 126, 127, 135, 146–47; planting, 15, 110, 121–**22**; staking, 20, 44, 49. *See also* citrus; pecans

trellises, 54, 67

turnips, 16, 49, 111, 116

V

vegetables, 16–18, 43; and aphids, 10, 150–51; bolting to seed, 19–20; cool-season, 78, 93, 107–12; fertilizing, 44–45, 147–48; planting bed preparation, 14–15; selecting, 154–55; winter, 16–17, 48–49, **108**, 111, 118, 131, **134**–35, 137–40, 152. *See also by type*

verticillium wilt, 107

verticutter, 29

vitamin B, 4, 43

W

wasp, cicada killer, 73–74

watering, 6, 18, 24, 43, 55, 64, 78, 93, 112, 126–27, 135, 147, **153**; deep, 68–69, 79–80; and fertilizing, 29–30; and split fruit, 94–95, 130; timing of, 69–70

watermelon, 37, 50, 89

watersprouts, 36

weed-killers: preemergent, 34-35, 85

weeds, 10–11, 15, 16, 34–35, 60–61, 66, 85, 89, 100, 131, 133

weevils, 32, 60, 116

whiteflies, 32

wildflowers, 6, 18, 123–24, 135, 142

willow, desert, 23

wind, 6, 20–21, **26**, 28, 86, 87, 112

working conditions, 63

Y

yucca, **46**

Z

zinc sulphate, 29–30, 41, 92

zucchini, 41–42

About the Author

George Brookbank was an extension agent in urban horticulture for the University of Arizona for more than 20 years. He is the author of *Desert Gardening, Fruits and Vegetables: The Complete Guide* and *Desert Landscaping: How to Start and Maintain a Healthy Landscape in the Southwest*. He lives and gardens in Tucson, Arizona.